Advance praise for *What to Eat When You Get Diabetes*

"Meet Molly, Sam, and Pete, and learn as they do from Carolyn Leontos's practical and on-target advice. All three struggle as they face the challenges of discovering they have type 2 diabetes and the changes they need to make in food and lifestyle habits. Thanks to Carolyn Leontos's suggestions, they begin the journey—as the reader can also—to healthful living."

—Marion J. Franz, M.S., R.D., C.D.E.

"Practical nutrition information with powerful health implications for people with type 2 diabetes. Drawing on her many years of experience as a registered dietitian and certified diabetes educator, Carolyn Leontos takes readers by the hand and leads them step-by-step toward the goal of good blood glucose control."

—Patti Geil, M.S., R.D., F.A.D.A., C.D.E.

"A fun and easy-to-read book on food and diabetes that gives information on enjoying appetizing food with tips to stay healthy."

—Karmeen Kulkarni, M.S., R.D., C.D.E.

"Comprehensive, practical, and extremely reader-friendly. No matter how your life has been affected by diabetes, this book will help you make sense of the wealth of nutrition information and advice available today, and it will answer your most pressing questions. It turns eating with diabetes from a dreaded experience into an enjoyable one."

—Sue McLaughlin, B.S., R.D., C.D.E.

What to Eat When You Get Diabetes

Easy and Appetizing Ways to Make Healthful Changes in Your Diet

Carolyn Leontos, M.S., R.D., C.D.E.

John Wiley & Sons, Inc.

New York • Chichester • Weinheim • Brisbane •
Singapore • Toronto

ISBN 0-471-38139-X

Printed in the United States of America

10 9 8 7

Contents

Foreword   vii
Acknowledgments   ix

Introduction   1

CHAPTER 1   The Basics of Eating with Diabetes   3

CHAPTER 2   What You Need to Know about
             Weight Loss   19

CHAPTER 3   Understanding the Food Pyramid Plan   41

CHAPTER 4   Learning That Calories Do Count!   57

CHAPTER 5   Watch Out for Portion Sizes   75

CHAPTER 6   Sugar and Carbohydrates: Not Forbidden
             Foods   87

CHAPTER 7   Figuring Fat: Which Kinds and
             How Much to Eat   103

CHAPTER 8   Read Labels   123

CHAPTER 9   Don't Give Up Your Comfort Food   139

CHAPTER 10 Eating Out Healthfully   155

CHAPTER 11 Eat Your Vitamins and Other Helpful
            Substances   169

CHAPTER 12 Balancing Food and Medication   181

CHAPTER 13 Finding a Dietitian   201

CHAPTER 14 Can You "Live" with Diabetes?   207

Appendix
   Diabetes Cookbooks   215
   Suggested Reading   219
   Helpful Organizations   223
   Useful Web Sites   227
Index   229

Foreword

For people with diabetes, choosing what to eat can be a challenge. The bottom line is to choose a variety of healthful foods that include a balance of types of foods, and to eat moderate portions. Easier said than done!

However, *What to Eat When You Get Diabetes*, designed for those newly diagnosed with type 2 diabetes, provides a step-by-step guide to making informed health choices, with an emphasis on making easy and appetizing changes.

Carolyn Leontos has all the credentials for preparing this nutritional guide. She has years of experience teaching individuals, groups, and even restaurant chefs how food affects health. She provides a very positive perspective for how to enjoy good food—focusing on what to eat, rather than on what to avoid. She combines practical tips with quotes from research, all presented in a concise, relaxed writing style.

Carolyn discusses all the key content areas of medical nutrition therapy for diabetes: a variety of meal planning approaches available for use by persons with diabetes; guidance for weight loss; how to use blood glucose monitoring results to study how foods affect your blood glucose; how to modify recipes (numerous wonderful recipes are included throughout the book); portion control; the basics on carbohydrate, protein, and fat; the roles of sugar replacers and fat replacers; ethnic foods; eating out in restaurants; food label reading, and even how to incorporate "comfort foods" into your daily meal plans.

Since no discussion of food for people with diabetes would be complete without including the interaction(s) between food and medication, Carolyn has provided an up-to-the-minute review of diabetes medications.

Finally, Carolyn has included a chapter on the role a dietitian can play in helping you learn to make healthful food choices, where to find a dietitian, and insurance reimbursement for a dietitian's services.

Indeed, this book is a great starting place for you and your family to learn how to choose appetizing and healthful foods. Soon, you will be adopting the healthful changes described in this book for yourself, as well as your family and friends. The result will be the confidence you gain in managing your health in new ways, along with great potential for improving your overall health.

—Anne Daly, M.S., R.D., L.D., C.D.E.
Director of Nutrition and Diabetes Education
Springfield Diabetes and Endocrine Center
Springfield, Illinois

Acknowledgments

Many people have contributed to this book, and I would like to thank each of them for their help. First of all, my husband, Art, for inspiring and supporting me throughout the process. My patients, who over the years taught me to question conventional wisdom, and to listen and respond to their individual needs. My reviewers, Patti Bazel Geil, M.S., R.D., F.A.D.A., C.D.E., Karmeen Kulkarni, M.S., R.D., C.D.E., and Hope Warshaw, M.M.Sc., R.D., C.D.E., whose constructive comments were invaluable. Nola Haynes, R.D., for her creative illustrations, and last, but not least, my editor, Betsy Thorpe, for her editorial expertise, which made this book better.

The nutrition information in this book is taken from several sources:

- USDA Nutrient Database for Standard Reference
- Nutrition Facts from individual food labels
- American Diabetes Association and The American Dietetic Association *Exchange Lists for Meal Planning* nutrient database and Nutritionist Four, First Data Bank, San Bruno, California.

What to Eat When You Get Diabetes

Introduction

This book is written to help people who have diabetes cope with one of the most challenging aspects of this disease—what to eat. It is the result of many years of teaching individuals who have diabetes how to develop strategies to deal with this disease. Some of these people suggested that I write a book in order to help the many people with diabetes who never attend a class or make an appointment for individual counseling. I hope that my experience as a Registered Dietitian and a Certified Diabetes Educator working with people who have just been diagnosed with diabetes will be beneficial to the reader.

Though this book is designed for individuals with diabetes, much of the information is also applicable to those who are at risk for developing the disease, those who are overweight or physically inactive, and those who may have an immediate relative with type 2 diabetes. It could also be useful for those who just want to lose weight, because a diet for a person with diabetes is also an excellent way to lose weight.

The book is designed to answer the questions I have been asked most frequently over the years. I have attempted to unravel some of the mysteries of good nutrition and address issues that are of concern to people who have diabetes.

Specific suggestions are given about the basics of food choices and preparation, as well as how to modify your favorite recipes. Questions are addressed such as: "Can sugar be used in a diabetic meal plan?" "How do I know which artificial sweetener is best?" "Is fructose a better choice?" and "What are sugar alcohols and are they safe to eat?"

Fat is another subject that comes up whenever food is discussed. Learn why it is important and why you can't just eliminate it from your diet and be done with it. Discover the facts about trans-fatty acids and understand the differences among saturated, polyunsaturated, and monounsaturated fats and why you should know what they are and why they are important.

Weight loss, meal plans, calories, portion sizes, healthful food choices in restaurants, vitamins, functional foods, and balancing food and medication are all addressed in this book. My hope is that the information provided will not only help you live with diabetes, but enjoy healthful eating as well.

CHAPTER 1

The Basics of Eating with Diabetes

Your doctor has just told you that you have type 2 diabetes. Diabetes is a serious, common, costly, but more importantly, a controllable disease. You are one of almost 16 million Americans who have this disease, approximately 6 percent of the population. As devastating as this news is to you, you are one of the more fortunate ones because you are among the 10½ million who have been diagnosed. Nearly one-third of the people with diabetes do not know they have it. Many people are diagnosed only when they develop problems from the complications of diabetes. Though you know diabetes is serious, costly, and all too common, you might question whether it is controllable.

Most of the people who have diabetes have type 2 diabetes, and those are the people for whom this book is written. About 80 percent of people with type 2 diabetes are overweight; consequently, weight control and food choices are the major problems and barriers to controlling diabetes.

Big questions that concern everyone are: "Do I have to give up my favorite foods?" "What about ethnic foods?" and "What can I eat in a restaurant?" Unfortunately, people with diabetes are often told what they cannot eat rather than what they can eat. This book will attempt to change that paradigm and accentuate the positive. It will show you how the food you eat can affect your health, and it will give you the information you need to make informed food choices.

Your doctor told you about all the implications of the disease: complications, medications, and diet. She told you that you had to take the steps necessary to get your blood glucose under control and recommended you purchase a blood glucose meter so that you could monitor it at home. She also recommended that you lose weight. Her receptionist provided you with some written information on self-monitoring of blood glucose, what you should eat, and the importance of exercise. The doctor also told you it would be a good idea to make an appointment with a dietitian to learn what you should and should not eat. The one thing you know for sure is that people with diabetes have to be on a special diet. You may have a panicky feeling in the pit of your stomach as you wonder what you can still eat for dinner.

Everything seems so overwhelming, and all this talk about complications is so frightening. The doctor said to lose weight, which is easier said than done. When you got home you read all the information you had received at the doctor's office. One pamphlet about food said that healthy eating is the first step in taking care of your diabetes, and the same kind of food that is good for the person with diabetes is also good for the whole family. You do not need special or diet foods. It also says that you can make a difference in your blood glucose through your food choices. You are beginning to think that maybe this isn't impossible after all.

What about Dinner?

Knowing that after leaving the doctor's office you would have little time to prepare dinner, you had planned to stop and pick up fried chicken. What should you do now? Especially since your doctor told you that you needed to lose some weight?

Stop and think about that fried chicken dinner. Is it your only option tonight or do you have other alternatives? One solution may be to remove and discard the skin and eat only one or two pieces of chicken instead of three or four. Another may be to select roasted, rather than fried, chicken. Or better yet, get out of the car and go into a market where you can buy a vegetable to eat with that chicken. Many times what we eat with the chicken—like biscuits, fries, and coleslaw—adds lots of calories. The easiest way to cut down on calories is to keep it simple. Vegetables are generally low in calories. Breading and deep frying or adding cheese sauce or butter adds calories. So to get started, select the vegetables you enjoy and try them without embellishment. If you cannot eat a salad without blue cheese dressing, try eating plain sliced tomatoes instead of a salad. If you cannot eat a dinner roll without butter, substitute bread sticks. In order to figure out what to have for dinner now that you have diabetes, you need to think about three things: variety, moderation, and balance. Integrate these principles into your life to simplify making food choices.

Variety

One of the easiest ways to healthy eating is to include a wide variety of foods every day. Everyone needs well over fifty different identified (and many yet to be identified) vitamins, minerals, and other nutrients from the food they eat. The greater the variety of food we eat, the better the chance we have of getting all the nutrients we need. Try foods you have never tried before to increase the variety you eat. The modern supermarket brings foods from around the world to our doorstep. Take advantage of the many new and different foods it has to offer. Try to taste a new food every week or every month. You may discover some new favorites.

When you think of variety, think about three or four different foods and different types of foods in each meal. Let's use an example. If you eat a turkey sandwich for lunch, you are eating two different types of food: bread and meat. You might make that a deluxe sandwich by adding several slices of tomato and romaine lettuce. You have added a vegetable and now have three different types of food. Add a glass of skim milk or 1 percent milk and you have made that sandwich a whole lunch that incorporates variety. If we do the same thing for dinner you could start with spaghetti and meatballs. You have two different types of food, three if the meatballs are in a tomato sauce. Add a salad and you have created a well-balanced meal.

Moderation

Your grandmother was right when she said you should not eat dessert until you ate your dinner. The reason she said this was because if you were allowed to eat your dessert first you would have filled up on dessert and not eaten your vegetables. If, on the other hand, you select foods that are high in fiber, such as fresh fruits and vegetables, whole grains and legumes or other beans, you will fill up on nutrient-dense foods and consequently will be less likely to overeat. You really are what you eat. The foods you eat do affect both your health and the way you feel.

It is also important to choose fewer foods that have fat, sugar, and salt added to them. If you believe that apple pie belongs in the fruit group you have some changes to make! For most people, cutting back on pre-prepared, processed, and convenience foods, which are high in fat, salt, and sugar, will be a big change. The important thing is to focus on the positive. Concentrate on good food and learn to maximize the flavor and the satisfaction you get from the foods you do eat. In my admittedly biased viewpoint, ripe, delicious fresh fruit is the best dessert of all. You may not agree, but give it a try, and you may be surprised at just how much you enjoy this treat.

The best part about the concept of moderation is that it eliminates "forbidden foods." If you think about eating moderate amounts of food, you can probably fit all your favorites in occasionally. Just knowing a food isn't forbidden makes it less attractive.

Balance

The concept of balance incorporates both variety and moderation. When we think of eating a "balanced meal" most of us visualize a piece of meat or fish, some type of starch like pasta or potato, maybe a green vegetable and a salad. The thing that we have to keep in mind is that it is important not only to include all types of food, but also to eat the right amount of each of these foods. For example, we need to eat a certain amount of protein every day. Most Americans get a lot more than they need. This is because we tend to think of meat or fish as the only sources of protein and have a skewed notion of how much we need. Five or six ounces of meat or fish (each day, divided among all your meals) is more than enough for most of us. So if you look at that balanced meal, you should see a piece of meat the size of a deck of cards, and the starch and vegetable should take up most of the space on the plate. Balance means eating the right foods in the right amounts.

When you look at the recommendations given in the Food Guide Pyramid, a guide for good eating, they seem pretty simple. Incorporating those changes into your daily routine takes a little more effort. Eating meals at regular times every day may be easy for you if you follow a regular schedule. It is a good idea to space your main meals five to six hours apart. Your body will handle food better if you give it time to digest one meal before you start another. Some people do well if they eat six small meals a day. The question then becomes what do we mean by *small*. That depends on whether or not you are trying to lose weight. If you need 1,500 calories in a day and choose to eat six small meals, a small meal is one that contains 250 calories. One small slice of cheese pizza with a thin crust contains 400 calories and a hamburger may contain 430 calories. It is pretty easy to see that six small meals are not an option for most people, as regulating portion size is very difficult, if not impossible.

Eating Habits

Most of us have overeaten on occasion. Thanksgiving dinner is one of those times. Usually the table is covered with good food, and we want to try some of everything. Then you get up from the table and feel just like the turkey at the start of the meal, stuffed. It takes all your energy just to watch the football game on television. Compare that to how you would feel if you had eaten a meal that included a moderate-size serving of lean meat or poultry, grains, vegetables, and fruit. Most of us would have more energy after the latter meal. However, we all must cope with the tendency to overeat on festive occasions.

If the only times any of us overate were on festive occasions we would not have too big a problem. But many people eat more than they need every day. For instance, most of us can claim charter membership in the clean plate club. We have been taught since childhood not to waste food, and therefore we may be inclined to eat whatever is on our plate or on the table, even when we are not hungry.

The important thing to remember is that food that is good for a person with diabetes is good for everyone. Do not use the excuse of "I cannot deprive my family of these high-calorie goodies." I remember working with a man who had diabetes and was the family cook. When he changed his eating habits to improve his glucose control his wife was delighted not only because it improved his health but also because she finally lost the fifteen pounds that she had been trying to lose for years. She lost weight merely by being supportive. She encouraged her husband to follow his meal plan and did not bring into the house foods he was trying to avoid. If you improve your food choices, you are making better choices for your family as well.

Food fuels our bodies, and our food choices do affect our health and our life. However, we must not ignore the fact that while we eat to live, we also eat to enjoy. Food is an important part of every social function in our lives. No

one has a birthday party or anniversary party without serving food. It does not matter whether you go to a Fourth of
July picnic or a fund-raiser for your favorite charity, food is
central to the event.

Food has also become big business. Approximately
twelve thousand "new" food products hit the market every
year. Food technology has been a boon in supplying numerous varieties of foods to every area of this country, and that
was unheard of just a relatively short time ago. We can eat
strawberries and asparagus all year long. We can eat fresh
fish in the middle of the desert, thanks to modern packaging, refrigeration, and transportation systems.

The miracles of modern food processing allow us to go
to the supermarket and purchase complete pre-prepared
meals; all we have to do is pop them in the microwave and
eat. Unfortunately, because they are pre-prepared we are
unaware of their ingredients and in many instances end up
consuming too many calories, too much fat, too much
sodium, and too little fiber. The frozen food industry provides a wide array of main dishes, vegetables, breads, and
desserts all ready to just heat and eat. The problem for
many of us is that we have become victims of this success.
It is so easy to pop that frozen pie or those cookies in the
oven because they are so convenient. So we tend to eat
these high-calorie foods much more often than we would if
we had to make them from scratch.

One of the easiest ways to make healthy eating simple
is to eat as many foods as possible when they are as close to
their natural state as practical. I am not suggesting we re-
turn to the hunter-gatherer era. What I do mean is that we
go back to the basic food and eat it the way it grows as long
as it tastes good that way. For example, a whole apple has
more fiber and more satiety value (it fills you up) than a

calorically equivalent amount of applesauce or apple juice (which is even more processed than the applesauce). Think about it: The apple takes virtually no preparation; all you have to do is wash and eat. If you are thinking about an orange or a glass of orange juice, try thinking about how many oranges it takes to make enough juice to fill a glass. If you drink the juice you may get more calories and carbohydrates than you should. Simply peeling and eating the orange is a much better choice.

Most of us are not going to make our own tomato sauce from scratch; however, we can make our own pasta sauce and thereby have control over the amount of fat and salt the dish contains. The same is true of many other foods. If you really want to know what you are eating, you need to do some basic cooking. Remember that even if you have never set foot in a kitchen, this isn't rocket science. If you can read and follow directions, you can cook.

Most people with diabetes will have to make some modifications in their eating habits. The most important thing to remember is that even though you have diabetes you can still eat food that tastes good and enjoy every bite. We acquire a taste for the majority of foods we eat when we are young and we can modify our likes and dislikes. If you doubt this fact, think about specific foods and beverages that you enjoy but that most kids will not touch. Conversely, kids have many favorite foods that you would never eat. Eating is a learned behavior. That fact puts you in control. If you learned to make poor choices, you can now unlearn them and relearn to make better choices. Part of the problem is attitude. It is true that you can teach an old dog new tricks. What is more important? Are you really willing to admit to yourself that you cannot change? Of course not. You are an intelligent person who is perfectly capable of accepting responsibility for and taking control of what you eat, your life, and your health.

It is very important to realize that virtually any type of food can "fit" into your new meal plan. If you cannot live without Mexican cuisine, do not panic. Italian, Greek, Mexican, Middle Eastern, and any other ethnic food are all possibilities. This book will concentrate on what you can eat rather than what you should avoid.

Some of the changes you can make in the way you eat to take care of your diabetes are straightforward. Make regular mealtimes a habit. It makes sense that if you eat breakfast you will not be "starving" by lunch. Or if you skip lunch, you are more likely to overeat at dinner. Eating regular meals and approximately the same amount of food at those meals each day can help you control your blood glucose.

If weight loss is your goal, and it is for the greatest majority of people with type 2 diabetes, food portion size and method of preparation become very important issues. You may be surprised to learn that the butter or margarine, sour cream and bacon bits, that you add to the baked potato have far more calories than the potato itself. If you have a lifetime membership in the "clean plate" club *now* is the time for change. It may be better to let food go to "waste" rather than to "waist." Variety, moderation, and balance are the keys to healthful eating. You will soon get "hooked" on fruits and vegetables the same way some people become "junk food junkies." The important thing is to consciously make food choices to promote your good health. Remember, good health and good glucose control are your goals, and when you achieve them weight will generally take care of itself.

Change Is Possible

I am going to introduce you to three people who are all patients of mine, all of whom, when diagnosed with type 2 diabetes, had the same question you have: "What Do I Eat Now?!?" See if you identify with any of them and their dilemmas.

Pete is the executive chef at a large hotel and casino in Las Vegas. He recently gained thirty pounds. Part of his responsibilities include making sure the all-you-can-eat buffet with its wide array of soups, salads, main dishes, and desserts looks and tastes great. How can he possibly change his way of eating? After all, he has to taste everything to make sure it is acceptable for his patrons. Can you imagine a worse scenario? Pete's problem is similar to that of many people who enjoy cooking and do so regularly. First of all he needs to become aware of what he is doing. "Tasting" does count and can add up to a considerable number of calories every day. In Pete's case he may want to use a smaller spoon for tasting so that he tastes, critiques, and moves on rather than eating a whole portion of something during preparation. The most important thing Pete can do is set realistic goals he can keep. It may be as simple as having a bowl of cereal in the morning so that he isn't starving when he arrives at work. That way he can taste what he needs to, rather than make a meal of "tastes" because he is hungry. Pete may also plan to take time to sit down and eat lunch. If he plans lunch he can have better control of what he eats than if he skips lunch and just "tastes."

Pete reminds me of many family cooks who sample so much in the kitchen that they have lost their appetite by the time they get to the table. One problem these "tasters" have is that tasting isn't satisfying. When you sit down to the table and eat, you know you have eaten a meal. When you pick in the kitchen it is easy to delude yourself into thinking that you really haven't had anything to eat. In the meantime you have consumed 300 or 400 calories as "tastes." If you are a "taster" your primary change may simply be to eat only at the table.

Molly is a working woman whose family was raised on carryout and convenience foods. She has struggled with her weight since the birth of her last child, 18 years ago. She gave up cooking when she started working full-time. For the past 20 years she has depended on carryout and convenience foods, which typically are high in calories, salt, and fat, to balance her schedule as a wife and mother. Molly is devastated with her diabetes diagnosis. Now she feels she will have to starve herself, because the doctor said she had to lose 75 pounds. Even if she had any desire to take up cooking again it was shattered by the thought of having to diet!

The first thing Molly needs to think about is how she can adopt some more healthful lifestyle habits that can be maintained long-term, rather than making weight loss a goal in itself. If Molly concentrates on healthy habits that will help her control her blood glucose, weight loss may end up being just one benefit that can last a lifetime. Molly's cooking skills may be rusty, but cooking is just like riding a bike: you really do not forget how to do it. She may be pleasantly surprised to find that over the last 20 years there have been lots of advances in cookware and cooking appliances that will make her new challenges easier and maybe even enjoyable.

Sam is a 73-year-old retired gentleman who has never had a weight problem and has just been diagnosed with diabetes. He just lost his wife. He never set foot in the kitchen except to talk to his wife. Sam is overwhelmed. His wife had always done all the food shopping and meal preparation in their home. Now that she is gone he has no idea of what to do. His doctor had recommended he make an appointment to see the dietitian, and Sam heeded that advice.

At his first appointment with the dietitian, she explained that the most important thing for Sam to do is to think logically. She had Sam sit down with paper and pencil and make a list of the things he enjoys eating for breakfast, lunch, and dinner. Sam thought about the way he has eaten all his life and listed the foods he commonly eats. He discovered there really are not that many foods on his list. The dietitian explained that most people repeat their food choices with regularity. She said that if you are suddenly faced with having to shop and cook for yourself, then breaking these new tasks down into parts will help you see that what seemed monumental has become manageable.

Sam looks at his list and sees that pretty much his whole life he has eaten cereal, juice, and toast for breakfast five days a week. Pancakes, waffles, bacon, and eggs were foods he only ate occasionally, on weekends and vacations. He has always eaten shredded wheat, Grape-Nuts or frosted flakes for breakfast. The dietitian asked Sam if he is happy with these cereals or does he want to try something new. He is happy with these, so now all that they have to do is determine if he is eating an appropriate serving size of each cereal because it is important to try to eat the same amount of food at the same time each day. When she showed Sam how to check the Nutrition Facts on the cereal boxes he finds that the manufacturer says two shredded wheat biscuits are a serving and they contain 160 calories. Sam says

he never eats more than one biscuit. One biscuit will provide 80 calories. If Sam wants to eat about the same number of calories from cereal each day he needs to find out
what the serving size will be for Grape-Nuts and frosted
flakes. The label says a serving of Grape-Nuts is ½ cup and
contains 200 calories. Sam could cut that in half and eat ¼
cup. He could look around the kitchen, find his wife's measuring cups, and use the one marked ¼ cup to scoop out the
serving of Grape-Nuts. When he does the same thing for
frosted flakes he also discovers he can have ½ cup of frosted
flakes for 80 calories. Sam puts about ½ cup of milk on his
cereal. He always drinks orange juice with his breakfast. He
needs to measure out his ½-cup portion and use the same
size glass every day. He also has one slice of toast with fruit
spread and black coffee with Sweet'n Low. If Sam eats this
same breakfast most days, his shopping and preparation for
this meal become very simple.

Sam and his dietitian have figured out that this meal
contains about 60 grams of carbohydrate. He learns that he
can substitute two small waffles with ¼ cup of reduced
calorie syrup for the cereal, milk, toast, and fruit spread. He
can still have his small ½ cup of orange juice. He can buy
frozen waffles, the kind you can put in the toaster. By
adding only two items to his shopping list that need virtually no preparation skills, he has added a new breakfast.
Once in a while he goes to a restaurant and eats a poached
egg and two slices of toast instead of the cereal and milk.
He always eats pretty much the same amount of food each
morning. That is important because if he eats too large a
breakfast his blood glucose will go up and will be higher
than it should be before lunch.

Sam isn't much of a lunch eater. Especially now that
he has to prepare his own meals and eat alone. When he
ate alone before he usually had a salami sandwich because

he didn't have to cook that. The dietitian spoke with him about how it is important to space his meals throughout the day for better glucose control. She told Sam that if he ate his largest meal or dinner in the middle of the day he could plan "leftovers" for supper or his evening meal. She suggested that Sam might be more motivated to cook for himself if he could prepare two meals at once. For example, he could prepare chicken breast, rice, and vegetables for lunch. If he cooked two chicken breasts he could slice the second one for a sandwich for supper. She suggested he learn to use his leftover meat for sandwich meals. This is a far better choice than buying salami or other high-fat luncheon meats.

She told Sam that it was very easy to steam fresh vegetables in the microwave. All he had to do was wash the vegetables well under running water, trim the waste, cut, and cook. Use microwave-safe cookware for all cooking and reheating. She explained to him that it is not safe to use plastics not designed for the microwave in a microwave oven because the high temperatures may cause chemicals in the container to leach out into the food. Cookware specifically designed for the microwave oven also allows steam to escape and not build up pressure in the container. It is very simple to steam vegetables in the microwave without adding any fat during the preparation. Sam left the dietitian's office feeling much better about his ability to cope with the changes he realized he must make. Sam's regular eating patterns will help him to control his blood glucose.

Basic Menu

All three of these patients of mine were interested in controlling their blood glucose through healthful eating, and wanted help in planning meals. The menu I am suggesting here will demonstrate how easy it is to prepare a delicious and satisfying meal at home. It is one that I think Pete, our professional chef, would enjoy yet is also low enough in calories to please Molly's physician and simple enough for Sam to fix. It can be prepared for one as easily as for a group.

Menu

Mixed green salad with balsamic vinaigrette
Poached or broiled salmon
Steamed spinach
Baked potato
Fresh fruit

This menu incorporates variety and balance. The moderation is up to you, and moderation is crucial if weight loss is your goal. Chapter 2 talks about weight loss strategies and a different approach to measuring progress.

What You Need to Know about Weight Loss

Statistics show that approximately 80 percent of people with type 2 diabetes are overweight or obese. If you are overweight, losing weight is a critical part of your diabetes therapy. So it would seem logical that if people with diabetes lose weight, this would solve the problem. The answer is not quite that easy. Weight loss is a very complex problem. The important thing for the person with diabetes to think about is how weight loss will affect their glucose control.

For years health professionals advised people to achieve their "ideal weight." That advice is shifting to recommending that people achieve a *healthy* or *reasonable* weight rather than strive for an illusive ideal number on the scales. There are a number of reasons for this shift in thinking. The bottom line for the person with diabetes is that they need to be concerned about keeping blood glucose, cholesterol, triglycerides, and blood pressure under control. Weight loss plays an important role in achieving these goals.

What the Research Says

Keep in mind that type 2 diabetes is a very complex disease and our knowledge about it is constantly growing. The results of research studies add a little or sometimes a lot to what we know about diabetes and weight loss. But any results have to be repeated over and over to prove that they hold up in all circumstances. While we get very excited over a breakthrough discovery and many times that breakthrough makes the evening news, we have to see if the "discovery" meets the test of time. We live in a world of instant communication and endless advertising. Health reporters on every major television network scan the scientific literature to find the latest developments, and preliminary results are reported as if they had stood the test of time. Researchers often appear to be presenting conflicting results. In reality, we are continually learning what works and what does not and adding to our overall knowledge.

Recent research on diabetes and weight loss does have some encouraging news for people who are overweight or obese. If you lose any weight it usually helps improve glucose control. For example, if you weigh 250 pounds and your "ideal weight" is 175 pounds, you might think you need to lose 75 pounds to improve your blood glucose number. In reality, your numbers may improve with even a 5 to 10 percent decrease in weight. So that means if you lose between 12 and 25 pounds you will probably see a big improvement. For all practical purposes, if you are overweight, *any* weight loss is beneficial. The important thing to do is measure your weight loss progress by looking at a different set of numbers. Instead of using a scale to measure your progress, use your blood glucose tests. If your blood glucose improves, the chances are your cholesterol and triglycerides will follow suit.

While there is still a lot we do not know, there is some evidence that restricting calories may be an important factor in improving glucose numbers for the overweight person with diabetes. What is most important is to determine how what you eat affects your blood glucose numbers. Once you start to think like this, it will make a lot more sense for you to check your blood glucose regularly and make food and activity decisions based on those numbers, rather than blindly following a restrictive diet.

Weight Loss Strategies

Think for a moment about the weight loss industry in the United States today. About 50 percent of women and 25 percent of men in this country are on some sort of weight loss diet. This is a multimillion-dollar industry. Many people go from one diet to another because the first one didn't work. In reality, it probably did work. If you lose weight the diet worked. Maintaining weight loss is another issue altogether. Years ago there was a diet fad that consisted of eating merely grapefruit and hard-boiled eggs. Did this diet work? Absolutely! Anyone who stuck to it lost weight. The problem is how long can you stick with the prescribed program? Think about it. How many days could you tolerate eating nothing but grapefruit and hard-boiled eggs? The one thing we know for sure is that losing weight is hard to do.

There are lots of weight loss programs available. In order to help understand how they work, how they are similar, and how they differ, some of the various programs are described in the following section. **The bottom line is that**

in order to lose weight you must use or burn more calories than you take in. How you do that and what that number is for you is determined by *your* wants and needs. Diets are like panty hose: one size does not fit all!! At present there appear to be two components that are essential for successful weight loss and maintenance. They are: (1) increasing physical activity and (2) modifying eating behavior. It is important that you keep in mind that you have shifted your emphasis from numbers on the scales to numbers on the blood glucose meter and that your goal weight should be determined by your blood glucose numbers.

Physical Activity

There are many different ways for people to successfully attain and maintain weight loss. Some follow a specific meal plan, others quit snacking between meals. The one similar thing is that all of these people increase their activity level. There are two sides to the weight equation. You can take in fewer calories, you can burn more calories, or you can do both. Those people who seem to be most successful are the people who do both. In addition to helping with weight loss in people with type 2 diabetes, increasing physical activity helps your body to use insulin more effectively. This can help you improve your blood glucose control.

It is important to note that I am talking about increasing physical activity rather than about exercising. What is the difference? For our purposes let us say that if you work up a sweat you are exercising; anything less than that is physical activity. If you wish to start an exercise program make sure you check with your physician first. It is also important to start slowly and work up gradually. Remember that you do not have to lift weights or run a marathon in order to see health benefits from increased physical activity.

I can already hear all the excuses about why you cannot be physically active. You cannot join a health club because they are too expensive, not convenient, or just plain intimidating. You live in a cold climate and can spend time out of doors only six months of the year. You work long hours, and it is too dark to walk before or after work. You have arthritis in your knees and it hurts to walk. I am asking you to think differently and creatively about how you might increase physical activity.

Think about the things you do on a daily basis and consider if you can be more active in doing these routine activities. One woman I knew started walking, rather than driving, to the mailbox at the end of her rather long driveway. You can always park at the far end of the parking lot when you go shopping. Not only will you reap the benefits of the extra walk, you may prevent a ding in a car door because you have parked away from the madding crowd! Everyday chores like running the vacuum or gardening count. Dancing can also contribute to your daily total. Even if you have trouble getting out of a chair, try arm and leg movements while sitting down. The most important thing is to think about what you can do, not dwell on what you cannot do.

Modifying Eating Behaviors

Behavior modification is an essential component of any successful weight loss program. It simply means making changes that support your efforts to make better food choices. You need to determine what kinds of things trigger overeating and make changes to alter those things and the consequent overeating.

One tried-and-true behavior modification technique is to grocery shop from a list immediately after eating. You are much more likely to resist impulse purchases if you are not hungry. If you make a list for the items you need, you will avoid multiple trips to the grocery store and not be tempted to buy foods you do not need. Most of us will not make a trip to the store to buy a snack food at an odd hour. However, if the cookies or chips are in the house they are harder to resist. If you exercise dietary discretion in the grocery store, it is much easier to exercise dietary discretion at home.

For many people the sight or smell of food is enough to melt all resolve. If you cannot resist a fresh doughnut from the shop you pass on the way to work each morning, alter your route. If you do not see or smell the doughnut shop, it is much easier to resist the doughnut.

If you always bake cookies with your grandchildren, start a new tradition. Do some type of craft project with them that they can use to decorate for the holidays. Take them hiking, walk the dog, or teach them to play a new board game instead. The thing they will remember forever is the time you spent with them. And if your health is better you will have more quality time to spend with them.

The most important principle in modifying eating behavior is to figure out what prompts you to eat. Then, alter the scenario so that you either remove the prompt or change the circumstance in some way so that you do not eat in response. Think about a party before you go. If everything there is going to be high-calorie, call the host or hostess and offer to bring "something." Make sure that what you bring is both lower in calories and delicious. Then you will have something to eat at the party that tastes good and leaves you satisfied.

There are two weight loss strategies—appetite suppressants and very-low-calorie diets—that you should never, ever under any condition attempt on your own. These are extreme measures that may be of benefit to some people. They should only be used under strict medical supervision. This is particularly important for people with diabetes.

Appetite suppressants are medications that help to control the appetite. These drugs may alter chemicals in the brain to decrease the sensation of hunger. The important thing to remember is they are drugs. Like any foreign substance we introduce into the body they may have side effects. Before taking these or any drug, it is important to look at the risk/benefit ratio and decide whether or not the risk is worth the benefit. It is also extremely important not to self-medicate. Do not take these pills unless you are under very close medical supervision. Every so often, a new medication is discovered that promises to be the weight loss panacea. Then a year or so later we learn about a downside and that drug is taken off the market. It is important to keep in mind that there is no magic bullet when it comes to weight loss. Even if an effective appetite suppressant is found, if you wish to maintain weight loss, it is still crucial to change your habits so that you maintain an equilibrium between the calories you consume and those you burn.

Very-low-calorie diets (VLCDs) are regimens that provide between 400 and 800 calories a day and usually result in very rapid weight loss. They can be what is called a protein-sparing modified fast, where you would eat that limited number of calories as very lean meat, poultry, or fish. Or they may be a liquid formula that is commercially prepared. These prepared products provide 100 percent of all essential nutrients. This type of weight loss therapy is recommended only for people who have a large amount of weight to lose, have no other significant health problems, and are willing to follow a behavior modification program after they have lost weight. **Do not try to treat yourself with an over-the-counter liquid diet!** It is extremely important that a physician and team of experts that may include a dietitian, nurse, and exercise specialist who are trained in the use of these diets closely supervise anyone who attempts to lose weight by following a VLCD. These programs always include behavior modification and physical activity. Since you have diabetes you also need a physician who will monitor your diabetes and adjust your medical therapy as needed during the weight loss process.

A common weight loss strategy for a person with diabetes is an **exchange diet**. This diet is individualized with calories determined for each person. It is based on the pamphlet *Exchange Lists for Meal Planning* available from the American Diabetes Association, which categorizes food according to its carbohydrate, protein, and fat content. The calories and other nutrients are divided throughout the day, and the meal plan is designed to help normalize blood glucose. The calorie level of this plan can be adjusted for weight **loss, gain,** or **maintenance**. This plan offers a great deal of flexibility in food choices. Usually a person with diabetes is referred to a Registered Dietitian to learn how to use this type of meal plan.

Calorie-counting diets allot a certain number of calories each day. These calories are usually divided among three meals and in some instances a snack. This regimen is very straightforward. You can consume a certain number of calories at each meal. It does not make any difference what foods you select to provide those calories, as long as you do not exceed that number. There are lots of books and pamphlets that break down the 1,000- or 1,200-calorie diets into meals that contain 3 ounces of chicken, ½ cup of rice and ½ cup of green bean. The problem is that when you get tired of the chicken and green beans then what do you do? If you restrict your calories you will lose weight. In order to keep the weight off, restricting calories must be an ongoing process. You end up knowing exactly how much chicken and green beans to eat, but when you are faced with lasagna or burritos, what do you do?

There is some new evidence that shows our ability to burn fat, especially from large meals, decreases as we age. Researchers from Tufts University say that older women who are in their fifties and sixties burn 30 percent fewer calories from fat from a 1,000-calorie meal than women in their twenties. Fat-burning ability for smaller meals was the same for both groups. This indicates that older people may be better off if they stick to several small meals each day rather than saving calories for a big splurge. I am sure you will have better blood glucose control if you space your calories, and it appears you will burn more of the calories you eat if you space your calories. So what is the problem? Simply keeping those more frequent meals small. If you are trying to stick with 1,500 calories a day, try to divide those calories into three meals and three snacks. You divide your calories into approximately 250 for breakfast, 400 for lunch, 500 for dinner, and 100 for each snack. I know that totals 1,450 calories, but it does allow a little latitude for the "approximately." If we translate that calorie breakdown into food, it might look like this.

Meal	Food	Calories
Breakfast	1 scrambled egg	75
	1 slice toast	80
	1 tsp. margarine	45
	½ grapefruit	60
	coffee or tea	
	Subtotal	260
Midmorning snack:	1 apple muffin*	115
Lunch:	2 ounces lean roast beef	110
	2 slices rye bread	160
	1 tsp. mayonnaise	45
	lettuce	0
	8 oz. skim milk	90
	Subtotal	405
Afternoon snack:	6 ounces light yogurt	90
Dinner:	½ cup spaghetti	80
	¾ cup meat sauce†	205
	1 slice Italian bread	80
	vegetable salad	25
	2 tsp. olive oil	90
	Vinegar	0
	1 medium-size fresh peach	60
	coffee or tea	0
	Subtotal	540
Evening snack:	½ cup homemade salsa‡	25
	6 baked tortilla chips‡	80
	Subtotal	105
	Total calories	1,515

*Recipe for apple muffins on p. 71
†Recipe for spaghetti sauce on p. 82
‡Recipe for salsa and baked tortilla chips on pp. 54 and 55

Low-carbohydrate diets are the subject of considerable debate. This is particularly true for people with diabetes, as carbohydrates have the most impact on blood glucose. If a diet is low in carbohydrate, it will be higher in protein and fat. This may cause problems, because too much protein can put an extra burden on the kidneys. Too much fat may result in cardiovascular or heart problems. Carbohydrate is essential for the body to use protein and fat properly. When we eat an adequate amount of carbohydrate our body digests food the way it was designed to. If we cut carbohydrate too much we do not metabolize fat and consequently excrete it. Certain tests that measure the ketones in our urine can show if we are excreting fat. The difficulty with trying to lose weight on a low-carbohydrate diet is that as soon as you eat a normal amount of carbohydrate you start to metabolize fat and regain all the weight lost. If you virtually eliminate carbohydrate, you lose weight. As soon as you begin to eat normal meals, which contain carbohydrate, you regain weight.

The premise behind the **fat gram diet** is that most of us get a relatively set percentage of our calories as fat. If we limit that fat, we will automatically eat less and consequently lose weight. Fat gram diets concentrate on limiting the fat you can eat. This is based on the premise that fat is more fattening than other nutrients, so if you limit your fat everything else will take care of itself. Typically there are no limitations on other nutrients. If, for example, you need 1,500 calories to maintain your target weight, you would take 30 percent of that number, or 450 calories of fat. Then divide the 450 calories by nine because there are nine calories in one gram of fat. That would equal 50 grams of fat, the amount you could eat if you were aiming for 30 percent or fewer calories from fat. If you wished to lose weight you might limit your fat to 40 grams or less each day. Hypothetically, you can eat as much protein and carbohydrate as you wish, because they are not as fattening as fat. Protein and carbohydrate have 4 calories in each gram. The problem is that if you eat enough calories from protein and/or carbohydrate, you will make up for the fat calories you did not eat and will not lose any weight. Another problem with counting fat grams is in order to know exactly how much fat you are eating, you must know exactly how everything you eat is prepared, and you must also know exactly how much you are eating. This is difficult even for the most diligent among us. Even if you do not exceed your fat gram limit it is easy to "override" the basic premise behind the diet. Some people do this by drastically increasing their intake of fat-free and low-fat foods. Even though they are eating less fat, they are eating more food and consequently more calories.

Some diet center programs, such as Jenny Craig, focus on **prepared meals**. In these programs you purchase food that is portion controlled to provide a specific number of calories. You follow a plan that tells you very specifically what to eat at each meal. You do not need to make daily decisions about what to have for dinner. Some people do well on this type of plan. These plans have you come in to their center on a regular basis to weigh in and for counseling. They also have classes that teach behavior modification techniques. Other programs focus on support group techniques to help clients lose weight and maintain that loss. Like other methods of weight loss these programs will work if you follow them.

Many people are more successful at maintaining weight loss if they have a support system. There are support groups for weight loss like Overeaters Anonymous. Many people with type 2 diabetes join these support groups.

What about You?

You may be asking yourself which of these strategies will work for you and how you can make changes. Let me give you an example. Remember Molly, the working woman who has struggled with her weight for years without long-term success?

Molly's doctor told her that her weight wasn't just a matter of appearance anymore, her health and well-being were at stake. Like many other women she had gained over fifty pounds since her twenty-fifth birthday. The doctor explained that the first thing they would try is to bring her blood glucose under control with diet and exercise. If that was not enough they could try medication, which would take the form of pills or insulin. He explained to Molly that eating right and exercise are part of the regimen for anyone with diabetes whether or not they need medication. In some instances it is enough and it is possible to save the money and the hassles involved with medication. Molly knew she *had* to lose this weight and yet she didn't know where to begin. She decided to follow her doctor's advice and get help from a dietitian. Molly is fortunate to have health insurance. It covers diabetes medical nutrition therapy prescribed by a physician.

At my office she was given a questionnaire on food frequency that asked how often she ate certain types of foods. She was also asked to write down everything she had eaten in the past twenty-four hours. Some of the questions were about her favorite foods. Molly hesitated to answer those, as she suspected once the "health care police" found out what she really liked they would tell her she couldn't have it anymore. Nevertheless, she answered the questions honestly, as she knew she had to get serious about weight loss.

The first thing I asked Molly was if she had ever tried to lose weight before. Molly replied by listing every diet that she could remember trying. She named several liquid plans, the grapefruit diet, fasting every other day, counting calories, low-protein and a fat gram diet. They had all worked for a time, but she always regained the weight. I told Molly that since none of those approaches had been successful we should work together to figure out what behaviors Molly can change so that she will lose weight and improve her health over the long term.

I asked Molly how much weight she wanted to lose. Molly said that she knew she was overweight but didn't want to lose too much, as her husband didn't want her to be skinny. I replied that it may be a good idea to establish some short-term goals that she could reach over the next couple of months, because the real goal is Molly's health, while appearance is secondary. I suggested that Molly consider blood glucose control a goal, rather than a specific number of pounds. The amount of weight to lose can be determined by blood glucose results. What is a reasonable weight for Molly? It is one that she can attain and maintain.

I explained how food affected blood glucose and that some foods raise it more quickly and higher than others. The amount of food eaten at one time also made a difference. Molly learned that she could discover how foods affected her blood glucose by testing herself after she ate those foods. I then saw that pizza was on the list of Molly's favorite foods. I suggested that the next time Molly ate pizza, she check her blood glucose two hours after so that she could learn what effect the pizza had. This was a new approach for Molly. She had never thought of trying to figure things out like this.

I told Molly that it would be a good idea to try this experiment on a weekend or other day off work. Then she would have enough time to do the experiment, and if her blood glucose was high or low she would be able to do something about it. I explained that Molly would soon become an expert and be able to adjust her food and activity to positively affect her blood glucose. Molly should feel as if she is in control, rather than the doctor or the dietitian. I told Molly that the person with diabetes is the most important player on the health care team. She is the one who really should be "in control." The health care professional can help, and different team members have different roles, but all decisions revolve around what the person with diabetes is *willing and able to do*.

This made a lot of sense to Molly. She remembered that the doctor had suggested that it might be a good idea for her to monitor her own blood glucose. She had bought the meter her doctor had recommended but not asked why she needed it. Now she was beginning to see how checking her blood glucose at home might have some value.

I gave Molly a pamphlet from the American Diabetes Association called *The First Step in Diabetes Meal Planning*. We discussed the importance of healthful eating and its importance in overall diabetes care. Molly had never given much thought to choosing high-fiber foods as a way to satisfy her appetite. I explained that food that required chewing was usually more satisfying in the long run than food that literally melts in your mouth. It was reassuring to Molly to learn that she did not need special food. The pamphlet had suggestions about how to eat. It emphasized what to do, rather than what not to do.

It occurred to Molly while driving home after our appointment that her worst fears had not come true. I had not given her a calorie-restricted diet. Instead of her favorite food becoming a no-no, it was the subject of an experiment. What behaviors was she willing to change? How could she solve her problems?

The week went quickly for Molly. She took a needle-work project to work so she would have something other than eating to occupy her break time. She ate breakfast at home two mornings and on those days was not even tempted by the doughnuts at work. She had ordered pizza on Sunday so that she could experiment and learn how it would affect her blood glucose. She checked her blood glucose right before the pizza was delivered. It was 180 mg/dl, not too bad considering it had been 280 mg/dl at the doctor's just ten days ago. She ate the pizza and checked her blood glucose two hours later. Molly was devastated—her glucose reading was 310 mg/dl. What could she do? She remembered that I had told her that exercise helped to lower blood glucose. She went for a brisk walk around her neighborhood and checked again when she came home an hour later. She was down to 280 mg/dl. Still too high, but at least beginning to move in the right direction.

When Molly returned for her next visit she brought her blood glucose records and her concern about what happened when she ate the pizza. I asked her how much pizza she had eaten. Molly responded that she was home alone for this experiment, so she ate the whole thing. But it was only a medium, not an extra large. Molly was very pleased that she had conducted this experiment on herself and was learning firsthand how food and exercise affected her blood glucose. It was impressive that Molly had taken steps to solve the high blood glucose problem. That was an important step in diabetes self-management and Molly should be proud that she had taken action to solve her problem.

We talked more about Molly's day-to-day activities and the part food plays in them. Molly now eats something at home for breakfast. At lunch, she either goes out with her coworkers or they order in. She and her husband normally eat dinner at home. It is common for either Molly or her husband to stop on the way home and pick up something for dinner like fried chicken, barbecued spareribs, pizza, or hamburgers and fries. They also tended to snack on chips and dip while relaxing and watching television in the evening.

I pointed out that the biggest problem seems to be in the evening, starting with dinner. Molly agreed, yet she shudders at the thought of cooking from scratch every night. I asked Molly to think of things that she could do to make better food choices, things that are practical, that she can stick with over the long term. She already started to eat more vegetables and that had not been too hard.

Since Molly and her husband like to snack in the evening, I suggested that Molly stock up on low-calorie snacks. Raw vegetables are great because they tend to be filling and you can serve them with a low-calorie salad dressing for a dip. I suggested that she try a variety of vegetables such as raw broccoli, cauliflower, zucchini, red, green, and yellow peppers. That way Molly and her husband will not get bored with celery and carrot sticks. I also suggested that Molly keep cut-up vegetables in the refrigerator, so that they would be easy to serve when she came home from work. These seemed like reasonable ideas that Molly was willing to try.

I recommended that Molly try the new place in town that has all sorts of prepared foods. Maybe she can buy roasted chicken instead of fried. She can cook a vegetable in the microwave, add a salad, and have dinner ready in ten minutes. She is also willing to start cooking on the weekends. I talked about cooking enough for several meals at one time. Package the food in meal-size portions and freeze them for later use. The important thing is for Molly to decide what she wants to do.

It seemed pretty obvious to Molly that she would have to make some changes. I suggested that Molly concentrate her efforts on one thing at a time. Molly knew that she needed to think about what she ate from the time she got home from work in the evening until bedtime. It seemed as if all she did was eat dinner, watch television, and go to bed. She was not sure how much she ate while watching television.

I suggested that Molly write down everything she ate from the time she left work until she went to bed, and that she needed to be honest with herself. She needed to become aware of what she is doing in order to figure out what she can change. Molly left the office with two short-term goals. She planned to modify one evening meal and write down what she ate in the evening at least three times. She also planned to continue to monitor her blood glucose twice a day.

When Molly returned for our appointment three weeks later she was really excited. She could hardly wait to share her blood glucose records with me. She said she had discovered that the amount of food she ate for dinner seemed to affect her blood glucose. She also had discovered that when she snacked on vegetables or light popcorn and diet soda her blood glucose was much lower than when she ate a bag of chips or nuts.

She brought her food records. She learned that merely writing down what she ate helped her to eat less. Molly was becoming very conscious of what and when she was eating, instead of just eating from habit. I asked Molly to concentrate on how she felt when she was hungry and how she knew when she was full. Eating only in response to sensations of hunger was a totally new behavior for Molly. She liked the idea of being in control of what she ate, rather than have the food control her. Since she was doing so well, we scheduled her next visit for three months later, but I told Molly she could call in the meantime, or come back sooner if she ran into any problems.

Over the course of the next three months Molly called a couple of times. She wanted to try pizza again but was afraid she would raise her blood glucose too high. I suggested that Molly order pizza for a meal when her husband was home. That way she would be able to enjoy a slice or two of pizza but would not be able to eat all of it. She might make a vegetable plate for a snack and a good-size green salad to start the meal. That way it would take less pizza to satisfy both Molly and her husband. She might also go for a walk an hour or so before she planned to eat. I said that if Molly checked her blood glucose after her walk, before she ate the pizza, and again two hours later she would have a good idea of how her blood glucose responded to the meal.

Molly followed the suggestion and called back after the pizza meal to let me know how she had done. Molly reported that she ordered the pizza for Saturday evening supper with her husband. In the past they had always eaten the pizza on the couch in front of the television. This time they shared the vegetable tray in front of the television. Since Molly had made a salad, she set the table and they ate it there. Molly did not want to put a pizza box on the dining table, so she served each of them a piece of pizza and kept the rest warm in the oven. Molly was amazed that after she had eaten two pieces of pizza she was full and really did not want any more. She was learning that she ate less when she ate at the table than she did in front of the television. Her husband ate the rest of the pizza, so there were no leftovers to tempt her later in the evening. This was amazing. They had shared a single pizza and were satisfied. Just a couple of months ago they each would have eaten a whole pizza. Adding the vegetables and salad made a difference. Molly checked her blood glucose two hours after her supper and it was 180 mg/dl. She was proud of herself. Molly was learning to solve her diabetes-related problems and enjoy her meals at the same time.

When Molly came back for her three-month follow-up visit, she was wearing an outfit that three months ago was too small for her. She was feeling and looking better than she had in several years. She and her husband were walking two miles a day. She reported that her physician was very pleased with her blood glucose. He had praised her progress and encouraged her to maintain her lifestyle changes. He told her that he wished all of his patients would take such active control of their health. He was pleased that he did not need to prescribe any medication at this time. Molly was particularly happy that he was looking at what she had accomplished. She was feeling better and had more energy. She knew she could continue her lifestyle changes.

The simple changes Molly made are ones that anyone could incorporate into their own lifestyle. It is important to decide what you are willing and able to do and to concentrate on one thing at a time. Once you feel comfortable with one change, decide on the next change you might make. Even small changes, like switching from regular soda to diet soda, can make a big difference in the long run.

Be assured that your food choices don't have to be boring. Chapter 3 demonstrates how to "fit" any food into healthful eating.

Self-monitoring blood glucose is a cornerstone of diabetes self-management. It is a way that individuals can check their own blood glucose on a regular basis to learn how food, physical activity, and medication affect their blood glucose. Several companies manufacture meters for home blood glucose testing. They all require a tiny drop of blood and give results in seconds. The devices used to obtain the blood make the procedure painless. Each meter operates just a little differently, so it is important to get individualized instruction on how to operate any meter you purchase. Some meters can interface with your computer, giving you the ability to easily track your blood glucose over time. You can even send your numbers to your health care provider over the Internet.

When you purchase a meter, the pharmacy or outlet should have a qualified individual to teach you how to use the meter. If you attend diabetes education classes or receive individual instruction from a diabetes educator, you will learn how to use your meter. If you have any problems, all meter manufacturers have toll-free numbers you can call for help. The number is usually found on the back of the meter.

Use your meter to check your blood glucose on the schedule you and your health care provider have agreed upon. You can also use it to see how a particular food or activity affects your blood glucose. Follow these steps:

1. Check blood glucose.
2. Record number.
3. Walk, exercise, or eat the food you want to check.

4. Check blood glucose 30 minutes after activity or eating.
5. Check blood glucose 2 hours (1½ hours after first check) after eating or activity.

The numbers will give you information on how your choices affect your blood glucose. Check with your health care provider for target blood glucose numbers to aim for when you are fasting and two hours after eating.
The American Diabetes Association (ADA) recommends that generally your fasting or premeal blood glucose be between 80–120 mg/dl.

ADA does not have an official recommendation for a postmeal blood glucose. However, most experts recommend it be less than 180 mg/dl.

CHAPTER 3

Understanding the Food Pyramid Plan

The Food Guide Pyramid was developed by the Department of Health and Human Services and the U.S. Department of Agriculture to help all Americans make healthful food choices. The pyramid was modified to make it more useful to people with diabetes. You can find the "diabetes pyramid" in *The First Step in Diabetes Meal Planning*, an American Diabetes/American Dietetic Association pamphlet (call 1–800–232–2383 for a free copy). Both pyramids illustrate what we should eat for good health.

What do I mean by that? Let's look at the diabetes pyramid. The largest part of the pyramid is at the bottom. Here we find basic, staple foods. The list includes grains, breads, cereals, beans, and starchy vegetables. Eat six or more servings from this group daily.

The next level of the pyramid is home to the rest of the vegetables and fruit. This includes fresh or raw, frozen, cooked or canned vegetables, fruits and berries. It also takes in juice, puree, and sauce. Eat two servings of fruit and at least three servings of vegetables every day.

The third level contains milk, meat, and others. Milk may be fluid or dried and this group includes yogurt. Both milk and yogurt contain protein, fat, and carbohydrate. Cheese is listed with meat and others rather than with milk because it contains the same nutrients (protein and fat) as meat. "Others" include poultry, fish, eggs, and peanut butter. Limit your meat to six ounces and select two or three servings of low-fat milk a day.

The tip of the pyramid houses fats, sweets, and alcohol. These are grouped together because all of us need to consider the amount of these we consume more carefully than items lower down the pyramid.

Foods that are grouped together have similar nutritional value. Milk and yogurt both have similar amounts of protein, carbohydrate, and calcium. The fat content of both of these foods depends on what has been left during processing. Meat, fish, poultry, cheeses, and eggs all contain protein and fat. The amount of fat can vary widely. Non-starchy vegetables are virtually all low in calories and good sources of vitamins and minerals. Fruits add fiber as well as vitamins and minerals. They also contain significant amounts of naturally occurring carbohydrate. The foods in the base of the pyramid also provide carbohydrate, fiber, and other nutrients.

As I mentioned earlier, an easy way to think about selecting healthful meals is to try to pick something from each of the bottom three levels of the pyramid for each meal. Develop your own meal plan so that you get the correct amount of food. It is easy; just divide the total food for a day into three meals. The number of servings from each group will vary according to individual calorie needs.

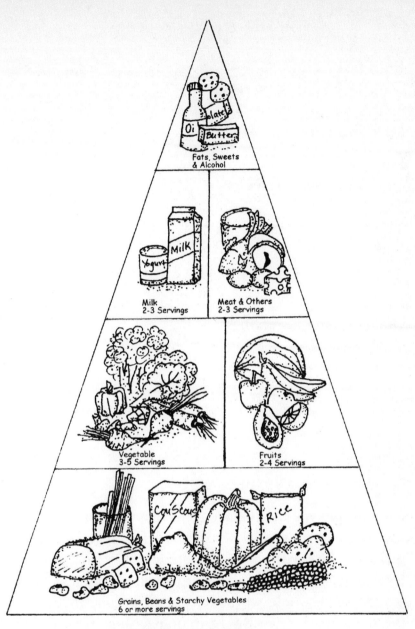

Diabetes Food Pyramid

Breakfast
Grain or starch: 1–2 servings
Fruit: 1 serving
Milk: 1 serving

Lunch
Grain or starch: 2 servings
Meat: 2 ounces
Vegetables: 1 serving
Milk: 1 serving
Sweets, fats, and alcohol: optional (use sparingly)

Dinner
Grain or starch: 2 servings
Meat: 4 ounces
Vegetables: 2 servings
Fruit: 1 serving
Sweets, fats, and alcohol: optional (use sparingly)

Snack
Milk: 1 serving
Grain or starch: 1 serving

For example you may decide to have a bowl of cereal with sliced strawberries and 1 percent milk for breakfast. The cereal comes from the base, the strawberries from the next level, and the milk from the third level. Or you may opt for orange juice, whole wheat toast, and yogurt. In this case the toast comes from the base, orange juice from the second level, and the yogurt from the third level.

Do the same for lunch. A hamburger on a bun with lettuce and tomato could meet the criteria. The hamburger bun is from the base, the lettuce and tomato come from the second level, and the hamburger patty comes from the third level. If the hamburger came from a restaurant or a fast-food outlet, you can request a dry bun, no mayonnaise or other sauce, and extra lettuce and tomato. That way you are in charge of how much extra fat you add to the sandwich rather than being at the mercy of the short-order cook. The extra lettuce and tomato ensures that you get a whole serving of vegetables, rather than just a half. Another choice may be a slice of vegetarian pizza. The crust comes from the base, the sauce and vegetables from the second level, and the cheese from the third level.

As you can see, planning dinner is manageable. Try stir-fry chicken and vegetables served over rice, which cover the bottom three levels of the pyramid. The rice is from the base, the vegetables from level two, and the chicken from the third level. A steak, baked potato, and salad are another choice. The potato is a starchy vegetable from the base, the salad covers the vegetables in level two, and the steak is from level three. If you add butter, margarine, or sour cream from the tip of the pyramid to the potato, you are adding fat, so remember to do so in moderation. It really is pretty easy to plan your meals this way once you get the hang of it. You can add low-fat milk and fresh fruit for a complete meal.

When it comes to snacks you may want to stick with something from just one level, like popcorn, or one thing from each of two levels, like cereal and milk, or fruit and yogurt or cheese. It is important to keep serving size in mind. This is not always easy to do in a society that continues to package foods in larger and larger containers and to promote the message that more is better.

Your individual caloric needs will help determine the number of servings from each of the food groups and how much leeway you have at the tip. Generally, the foods found in the top half of the pyramid are higher in calories than those found in the bottom half. For example, foods found at the base of the pyramid such as a small potato or $\frac{1}{2}$ cup of whole kernel corn each contain about 80 calories. If we go to the tip, a comparatively tiny teaspoon of oil, butter, or margarine contains 45 calories. An apple, even a large one, may contain 100 calories, while a piece of apple pie is going to be closer to 400 calories. Keep in mind that when you make pie from the apple you have "promoted" that fruit from the second level to the tip.

Many people with diabetes are able to learn how to make appropriate food choices and keep their blood glucose in good control by using *The First Step in Diabetes Meal Planning* as a guide. If you are able to do this, *The First Step* may well be the only step you need to take.

Do Ethnic Foods Fit?

The Food Guide Pyramid fits every culture. If you wish, it is easy to include ethnic foods in your meal plan. You can do this regularly or infrequently, depending on your tastes and mood. All you need to do is look at where these foods fit into the pyramid. In many instances when people in the United States speak of ethnic foods they are referring to ethnic restaurant food, which may typically be high in fat. If we look at the foods eaten in other countries we see that almost all food can easily fit into the diabetes food pyramid.

Mexican

A corn tortilla and serving of rice are just as much a part of the base of the pyramid as a small potato and slice of whole wheat bread. A soft chicken taco easily meets our criteria for the bottom three levels. The tortilla comes from the base, the vegetables from the second level, and the chicken from the third. Frijoles *cocidos*, better known to most of us as cooked beans, fit in the base of the diabetes pyramid. Chayote (a squash), jicama (a root), and nopales (a cactus) can be added to expand your vegetable list. Jicama, a crisp vegetable with a mild chestnut flavor, and nopales, which taste a little like green beans, both make great additions to a tossed salad. If you are a salsa fan, remember its main ingredients are vegetables, so a ½-cup serving is a vegetable. Avocados, because of their fat content, rise to the top of the pyramid. This doesn't mean you can't eat them; it merely means you need to watch your portion size when enjoying them or the guacamole prepared from them. Remember, if you have a ½-cup serving of guacamole, you are eating about 200 calories, while a ½-cup serving of home-made salsa is only about 25 calories. Aqua fresca is a beverage made from fruit juice or fruit puree, water, and sometimes sugar. It belongs in the fruit group. Like fruit juice, it contains calories, so you will want to limit your portion to a moderate amount.

Café con leche contains about half milk and half coffee and is a part of the milk group. It may contribute a significant number of calories, depending on the type of milk used in preparation. If you enjoy this beverage and wish to make it a part of your regular meal plan, consider preparing it with 2 percent or 1 percent milk instead of whole milk and sweetening it with a noncaloric sugar substitute.

Soul Food

The term "soul food" clearly conveys the concept that food does more than nourish the body; it lifts the spirit as well. Many times we associate this cuisine with fat, salt, and sugar, but with just a little modification of ingredients and method of preparation it fits the pyramid model very nicely.

Traditional favorites like yams, beans, rice, black-eyed peas, cornmeal, and grits take their rightful place at the base of the pyramid. Hopping John, a mixture of black-eyed peas and rice, is a healthful entrée. Could these heath benefits have contributed to the folklore that eating this dish before noon on New Year's Day would bring good fortune all year long?

Greens, all kinds of them, belong on the next level of the pyramid, as a soul food meal is not complete without collard, beet, or turnip greens. They can be cooked with onion and garlic instead of seasoning meat or fatback. Okra, onions, and tomatoes are other staples of soul food cooking found on this level of the pyramid.

Pork, chicken, and fish are the most common meats in this cuisine. Switch from deep or southern fried chicken or fish to the oven-fried variety as a lower fat alternative. Trim the visible fat from the chicken or pork before you add it to a recipe. Milk does not hold a predominant place in soul food cooking, probably because of the high incidence of lactose intolerance among blacks. You will find it is used in cooking, but not generally served as a beverage.

Lard, fat, and molasses are key ingredients found at the tip. Remember to use them sparingly and use herbs and spices instead to enhance the flavors. Garlic, onions, peppers, marjoram, oregano, sage, tarragon, cinnamon, cloves, cardamom, cumin, and ginger all contribute to making soul food that warms the heart and the soul.

Chinese

One of my very favorite dishes in a Chinese restaurant is war wonton soup. This is made with chicken broth, wontons, pork, shrimp, water chestnuts, bamboo shoots, green onions, and broccoli. The wonton wrappers are wheat based and meet our bottom-of-the-pyramid criterion. Water chestnuts, bamboo shoots, green onions, and broccoli are the second-level choices; pork, shrimp, and egg white come from the third level. All of these ingredients are cooked in water or broth, making a large serving of this soup an unusual and delicious low-fat meal. Or you could have a small cup of this soup to start a Chinese meal. Steamed dumplings, one version of dim sum, are another example of pyramid eating, Chinese style. Steamed dumplings may have a flour-based wrapper and be filled with a mixture of meat, poultry, or seafood and vegetables.

Chinese food offers lots of choices. Like so many other cultures, what we consider ethnic food in this country has been adapted for the American palate. What the natives eat is usually higher in naturally occurring carbohydrate and lower in fat than the special in the local Chinese restaurant. Many foods are steamed, rather than fried. Or if they are stir-fried they may be cooked with very little fat. Rice is a staple in the Chinese diet. It is eaten with virtually everything and is found at the base of the pyramid. Vegetables play a prominent role. Bamboo shoots, water chestnuts, mung bean sprouts, soybean sprouts, and black mushrooms are among the wide variety of foods listed in the vegetables group. Typical fruits eaten in China include star fruit, litchi, kumquat, mango, papaya, and persimmon.

Meat, fish, and poultry are usually eaten in small amounts. They take a secondary role in this cuisine. If a stir-fried dish includes meat, it is cut into small strips and combined with lots of vegetables. This fits nicely with our pyramid concept of smaller servings of foods from this group. Tofu or soybean cake is also found in this group.

Soy milk belongs in the milk group. You can drink it as a beverage, pour it on cereal, or use it as an ingredient in many recipes. Soy milk is a wonderful alternative for people who suffer from lactose intolerance.

Typical Chinese foods found at the tip of the pyramid include sesame seeds, sesame seed paste, and coconut milk. These foods add unique flavor and can be used sparingly to suit your taste.

Italian

Everyone knows that you can't eat Italian without eating pasta. It is the basis of many delicious Italian foods. And yes, it does fit at the base of the pyramid. The names of pastas vary depending on their shapes. It doesn't make any difference if it is mostaccioli or linguine; all of it is made from grain. Lots of other foods prominent in Italian cuisine also fit in the base of the pyramid. Polenta is made from cornmeal and risotto from rice. Garbanzo beans, sometimes called chickpeas, as well as other varieties of dried beans, fit in this category.

Sauces for pasta vary from marinara, the classic Italian red sauce; to Bolognese, traditional meat sauce; to Alfredo sauce, made with heavy cream and butter. Their ingredients determine their place on the pyramid. Marinara sauce is classified as a vegetable, unless the chef was heavy-handed with the olive oil; then it becomes vegetable and fat. Bolognese sauce is made from tomatoes and meat so fits in two groups, and the ingredients for Alfredo sauce come from the tip of the pyramid.

Zucchini, eggplant, tomatoes, squash, artichoke, escarole, and curly endive are all vegetables commonly associated with Italian food. If you prepare these foods yourself you can determine the amount of fat, if any, that you add. If someone else prepares these vegetables, be on the lookout for added fat. Peaches, pears, apples, figs, and grapes are found among the delicious fruit selections.

Fish and seafood are plentiful in Italy and prominent on Italian menus. Poultry of all varieties and cheese are also important food choices. Anchovies are frequently included on an antipasto tray. Though they are seafood, they are canned in oil, which provides more calories than the fish.

Olives and olive oil are among the selection of choice for the tip of the pyramid. They play a significant part not only in Italian cuisine but also in that of all the Mediterranean countries. In Italy, wine is frequently served with a meal. This, too, would be a selection from the tip, adding calories but very few nutrients.

Greek

Greek cuisine encompasses the top and the bottom of the pyramid. Olive oil, bread, and wine all are prominent in Greek mythology. The ancient traditions of the Greeks hold a good lesson for all of us. Overindulgence was the downfall of the Greek civilization.

When we look at traditional Greek foods it is easy to see where they fit in the pyramid. Rice, as pilaf and as an ingredient in many dishes, particularly stuffed grape leaves and other stuffed vegetables; dried beans and peas; and breads all make up the base. All fruits and vegetables are popular in this culture. Vegetables are frequently the centerpiece of the meal. As a matter of fact, the Mediterranean Diet, frequently touted as beneficial in preventing heart disease and cancer, is based on foods placed in the bottom half of the pyramid. A vegetable casserole of eggplant, zucchini, onions, peppers, and tomatoes fits perfectly in the vegetable group. Mint leaves, grape leaves, and cucumbers provide flavors that are traditional in this region.

In Greek cuisine fish and shellfish are the mainstay of the meat and others group. This is logical when we look at the geography of the region. The mainland is a peninsula and the country encompasses many islands. Consequently fishing plays an important part in the economy of the country as well as the diet of its inhabitants. Lamb also plays a very important role. Yogurt is as popular as milk and used in many recipes as well as eaten plain.

Foods found at the tip include honey, nuts, sesame seed paste, which may be called tahini, olives and olive oil, and wine. Learn the value of moderation in all things, and remember this lesson of the Greek civilization when enjoying this fine cuisine.

Indian

The region of Southeast Asia where India is located includes Pakistan and Nepal and the cuisine of all of these countries is similar. It is not surprising that spices and condiments heavily influence the foods of this region. Rice and wheat are important grains in the Indian diet and one or the other is eaten at most meals. *Naan*, a bread baked in a clay oven, and *phulka*, an unleavened bread, are examples of traditional foods that belong in the grain group. Lentils, used in many dishes such as dhal, and *idli* are also a mainstay of this group. Vegetables popular in this region include eggplant, okra, cucumber, and bean sprouts. Guava and mango are traditional fruits of this region.

The traditional diet of the people of this region of the world is plant based, and lentils and other legumes are frequently used in place of meat. Chicken, poultry, and fish are found in the meat and others group. Milk is usually not consumed as a beverage but used to make yogurt, buttermilk, and desserts. Most milk-based foods would be combination foods and fit into both the milk and other categories. Oil and sugar are found at the tip of the pyramid. Frequently they are ingredients in many traditional dishes, making that food a combination of two or more pyramid groups.

The Lesson of the Pyramid

By now it should be apparent that all foods can fit into the pyramid scheme of things. The most important thing to remember is that what you, or the cook, does to the food makes the difference. If you add fat to food, as in deep-frying, or rich sauces you will increase the calories significantly. For example, you can have pasta for dinner. If you top it with marinara, a plain tomato sauce, it may contain 200 calories. If you select Bolognese, a meat-based tomato sauce, it may provide 300 calories, and Alfredo, a butter and cream sauce, tops out at 500 calories, all for the same size serving.

Food can be prepared with a variety of seasonings to enhance its flavor. Frequently, the ingredients that offer the most flavor—like garlic, onions, peppers, hot sauce, herbs, and spices—add few calories. Fat is the ingredient that adds the most calories. Food can also be prepared in a manner that either reduces or increases its fat and caloric content. When you are preparing a meal ask yourself whether the method you are using adds or cuts the amount of fat in the finished product. Most of the time seasonings contribute lots of flavor but add few calories.

If you choose to select and prepare your meals pyramid style, you can incorporate a wide variety of foods and cuisines into your daily regimen. You can savor the flavors of all kinds of foods and never feel deprived while maintaining good control of your diabetes.

Snacking with the Pyramid

Plan snacks, don't just let them happen. If the thought of eating three servings of vegetables seems impossible to you, try thinking about having one of them for a snack. Raw vegetables with a low-calorie dip make a great snack. It is a good idea to clean and cut up raw vegetables when you bring them home from the grocery store. If they are readily available, you are much more likely to eat them. Many markets sell raw vegetables that are "table ready." All you have to do is serve and eat. They cost more but may be worth it in the long run. Vegetables are low in calories and tend to take the edge off your appetite if you eat them as an appetizer.

Tortilla chips and salsa can be planned into your day as easily as graham crackers and milk. All it takes is a little imagination and foresight. Baked tortilla chips are a starch choice, found at the base of the pyramid. Salsa is a vegetable. Together they make a creative, delicious snack you can enjoy all by yourself or with a roomful of friends. Besides they are, or can be, low in fat, cholesterol, and sodium. But I probably shouldn't tell you that. If you are one of those who believes if it is good for you it won't taste good, I am spoiling all your fun! Try the recipes I have included in this chapter. Snack and enjoy guilt-free snacking.

Salsa

Servings: 6

INGREDIENTS

2 small jalapeño peppers
4 medium-size red, ripe
   tomatoes
1 small onion

½ tsp. salt (optional)
¼ cup fresh cilantro,
   chopped

METHOD

Wash peppers, place them in a small microwave-safe container, and microwave on high for one minute. Cut tomatoes and onion into quarters. Put all ingredients into the bowl of a food processor fitted with the steel blade. Put the cover on and process for three or four seconds. Remove the cover and check for fineness of chopping. Repeat process until you have the desired consistency. Put salsa into a tightly covered container and chill until ready to use. If you double this recipe, process the salsa in batches. Do not overload your food processor, as it will not function efficiently. If you do not have a food processor, you can chop all the ingredients by hand using a sharp knife and a cutting board.

Makes about three cups, six ½-cup servings.

NUTRITION FACTS

Serving size: ⅙ of recipe,
   about ½ cup
Vegetable exchanges: 1
Calories: 24   Calories from fat: 0
Total fat: 0 grams
Saturated fat: 0 grams
Cholesterol: 0 milligrams

Sodium: 202 milligrams
   (with salt)
Sodium: 9 milligrams
   (without salt)
Carbohydrate: 5 grams
Dietary fiber: 1 gram
Sugars: 3 grams
Protein: 1 gram

Baked Tortilla Chips

Servings: 6

INGREDIENTS

6 corn tortillas (use one tortilla for each serving)
warm water
salt (optional)

METHOD

Put warm water into a bowl large enough for a tortilla to lay flat. Using tongs, immerse tortilla into water for two or three seconds. Remove, hold with tongs to allow to drain briefly. Place on cutting board and, using a sharp knife, cut into six pie-shaped wedges. Put wedges on a baking pan with a nonstick finish. Bake in a hot oven, 450–500° F., for three minutes, turn, and bake three or four more minutes until crisp.

N O T E

Use corn, or fat-free flour tortillas. Corn tortillas are virtually fat free, as no fat is used in their preparation. Regular flour tortillas are prepared with fat, in many cases lard. Traditionally tortilla chips are made with corn tortillas.

Check label for Nutrition Facts.

An 80-calorie serving equals 1 carbohydrate choice.

Using the food pyramid, it is easy to see how your favorite foods fit into your personal meal plan. Chapter 4 provides more information on how to cut calories, without cutting flavor, from these foods.

Learning That Calories Do Count!

Sometimes I think weight loss has overtaken baseball as the great American pastime. It seems as if everyone you meet is overweight and on some kind of a weight loss diet. How can you judge whether or not the latest best-seller diet book is any good? There is no magic to weight loss, and if it sounds too good to be true it usually is! In chapter 3, you learned that in order to be successful at weight loss you should increase your physical activity and modify your eating behavior. That is one of the first things to look at when you are trying to determine if a weight loss book is worth reading. Does your best-selling book address these issues or is it just more hype? All health books have disclaimers. There are lots of diet plans and most of them promise phenomenal results. Which one should you try? One advertises losing ten pounds in just one week. Another has "after" pictures of people who really look good. Do you ever wonder why there weren't any before and after pictures of the same person? There are just too many plans to pick from. How can you figure out which one will work?

Stop and think about how many times you see a report about the latest research on weight loss on the evening news' health report, which has somewhere between 30 and 90 seconds to give all the facts about any research study. It may have been a 3- or even 10-year study, yet the most the reporter can do is give one or two simple facts. Research studies are very complex, and there is a lot more to the results than can be given in such a brief report. One or two facts may be blown all out of proportion and the important concepts may be left out.

Sometimes creative writers or celebrities may take one or two concepts from a complex study and develop the latest "miracle" diet plan. The admonition "buyer beware" is an important one to remember before spending money on any weight loss program. The key to losing weight is that you must watch your calories and burn more than you consume. Some diet plans may be easier to follow than others, but weight loss is hard work and calories do count.

Why Count Calories?

Webster's Collegiate Dictionary says a calorie is the amount of heat needed to raise the temperature of one gram of water one degree centigrade. While this is correct, for our purposes, a calorie is the term we give to the energy produced by food in the body. All the food we eat (with the exception of water or a zero-calorie diet soda), no matter where it comes from, provides calories. Any food we do not use for energy is stored in our body, primarily in the form of fat or triglycerides. If an individual consumes more food than their body uses to support metabolic and activity needs, then that food is stored as fat for future use. This very efficient system has been keeping the human race in existence through times of famine and plenty. In the times of the hunter-gatherer, people would gorge when food was plentiful and the body would store the excess and use it when food was not available. If food is always available and at the same time continually stored by the body for future use, it is obvious that the storage depot (body) must get larger to accommodate this fat.

It is critical to understand that if you eat more food than your body needs to function then that food will be converted to fat for storage. Protein and carbohydrate are broken down and converted to fat for storage. Fat is stored as fat.

The first thing you need to know is that fat contains over twice as many calories ounce for ounce, or in metric terminology gram for gram, than either protein or carbohydrate. Fat contains 9 calories per gram, while protein and carbohydrate each contain 4 calories per gram. Most foods are a combination of fat, protein, and carbohydrate. Some foods, like 2 percent milk, contain significant amounts of all three nutrients. Others like bread are mostly carbohydrate, with just a little fat and protein. Meat, fish, cheese, and eggs contain protein and fat; and it is usually intermingled, with eggs being the exception. Egg white is pure protein, and the yolk is fat. Very few foods contain only protein or carbohydrate. Fat is much more available in a pure form. Some foods we think of as being high in protein are really high in both protein and fat, so you may be surprised to learn that a steak, even a lean one, has on average 7 grams of protein and 3 grams of fat per ounce. That means that the steak provides 28 calories from protein and 27 calories from fat in each ounce. I ask you: is the lean steak high in protein or high in fat?

What about Fat?

In practical terms, butter on bread can contribute more calories than the bread, as fat is a concentrated source of calories, so just a little bit can add a lot of calories. Another important fact is that from a caloric perspective, fat is all the same. **Olive oil has the same number of calories as lard**, and although they contain different kinds of fat, they all have 9 calories per gram. Olive oil contains a large percentage of monounsaturated fat and is considered beneficial, so consequently, the tendency is to use it liberally. But you need to remember that it is not calorie free!

Fat adds flavor to food. Cuisines from different parts of the world are based on or influenced by the type of fat that was available and used when these cuisines were developed. Olive oil has had a strong influence on Mediterranean food, and chicken fat plays an important role in kosher cooking. For years, homemakers throughout the United States carefully saved bacon drippings and "recycled" them in many foods. The same may be true of traditional foods in your family. You may believe that if you do not use the tried-and-true source of fat the food will not taste right. This is just not true.

The consistency of fat plays an important role in some foods. Flaky French pastry depends on very cold sweet butter to impart the flaky texture as well as the delicate flavor. Substituting vegetable oil for butter would yield a very different end product.

Fat also helps keep food from sticking to the pan. There are a lot of recipes that date from the days when cooking utensils and equipment were much more primitive than they are today—for instance, your grandmother may have cooked on a woodstove in a cast-iron pan. It was difficult to control the temperature, so lots of fat in the pan helped make sure the food did not stick or burn. Nowadays accurate thermostats and nonstick cookware alleviate the need to use the same amount of fat to prevent sticking.

Is Fat-Free the Answer?

There are an increasing number of fat-free and low-fat items on the grocery shelves these days. If you have diabetes then the question is how these foods fit into your overall meal plan. Will they help you lose weight? Maybe. Will they affect your blood glucose control? That depends.

When most of us see a fat-free product, we assume that the food so advertised is also low calorie. That is not necessarily true. When fat is removed from a food it may be replaced with another ingredient that contributes an equal number of calories to the food. For instance in a baked product, fruit puree can be substituted for some or all of the fat, and you need to be aware that fruit puree is not low in calories. If you eat a 300-calorie serving of a fat-free dessert in addition to your meal it will not help you to lose weight and it will raise your blood glucose. If on the other hand you select a 100-calorie serving of a fat-free food in place of a 150-calorie full-fat version of the same food as a part of a meal, it will help with weight loss. If you cut down on fat without substituting other sources of calories, you will probably lose weight. As far as your blood glucose is concerned, you will need to test and see for yourself.

There is no easy answer to the low-fat, fat-free debate. It depends on you. If you eat a box of fat-free cookies because you think they are acceptable, you are deluding yourself. If you eat one regular cookie and are satisfied, that may be the better choice for you.

Food is made up of 3 major nutrients: carbohydrate, protein, and fat. Although most foods contain a combination of nutrients, this list groups foods according to the nutrient that contributes the most calories to the food.

Carbohydrate Foods
Fruit
Fruit juice
Vegetables
Dried beans
Pasta
Bread
Cereal
Regular soda
Candies and other sweets

Protein Foods
Lean meat
Chicken and turkey
   without skin
Skim, nonfat or 1 percent milk
Egg white

Fat Foods
Butter
Margarine
Lard
Oil
Olives
Avocados
Meat, marbled,
   untrimmed
Duck and goose
Chocolate candy
Pastries
Cream
Whole milk
Egg yolks

Carbohydrate and Protein

Carbohydrate does have a major affect on blood glucose. The amount you eat should be determined by a nutrition assessment, that is, an evaluation of the food you eat and its relationship to your health, by a professional, usually a registered dietitian. It is important that people with diabetes keep this in mind when selecting food. How much carbohydrate should a person with diabetes eat? That depends on blood glucose and triglyceride goals.

Carbohydrate is the nutrient that is the major source of energy in the diet. It also is essential for the proper metabolism of protein and fat. Foods like fruit, vegetables, beans, bread, cereal, and pasta are mostly carbohydrate. We all need to eat enough carbohydrate to metabolize our food normally. If your blood glucose is out of control you are probably getting more carbohydrate than you need. Health professionals debate about how much carbohydrate you should eat. Some researchers recommend 40 to 45 percent of calories from carbohydrate; others say you should get 75 to 80 percent of calories from carbohydrate. Recommendations to eat specific percentages of calories from carbohydrate should always be based upon your individual needs. The most important thing to look at for someone with diabetes is blood glucose control. If your blood glucose is too high, it may be the result of eating too much carbohydrate.

Experts recommend that most carbohydrate choices should be from naturally occurring sources, such as grains, fruits, and vegetables. Refined carbohydrates such as pastries, candies, and other sweets should be eaten only in moderation. This is good advice for everyone, whether they have diabetes or not. It is not recommended that you virtually eliminate carbohydrate.

The recommendations of how much protein a person with diabetes should eat are similar to those for the general public. Adults need $\frac{8}{10}$ (0.8) of a gram of protein for each kilogram of body weight. That means an adult who weighs 154 pounds needs 70 grams of protein a day. Each ounce of meat, fish, or poultry contains 7 grams. Every ounce of milk has 1 gram and a slice of bread has 3 grams of protein. If you eat a sandwich with 2 ounces of turkey and a glass of milk, you are eating 28 grams of protein. Most of us get more protein than we need each day.

The best protein sources are those that are low in fat. Lean meat, skinless poultry, poached or baked fish that has been prepared without added fat are good choices. Beans, peas, and other legumes, again prepared with little or no added fat, have the added benefit of fiber along with the protein.

Food Choices

Everyone is looking for an easy way to lose weight. There is no easy way! We know that activity and exercise play a big part in weight loss and weight maintenance. However, these benefits can be overcome if we consume excess calories. Weight control is a complicated issue that involves more than just willpower. There are a lot of things to consider. For people with diabetes, calories is just one of them.

You do need to look at food choices. In this country, foods high in fat and calories are readily available. These foods are inexpensive and marketed through every available means. Not only can we get a high-fat lunch at a moderate cost, we do not even need to get out of the car to do so. Compare that scenario to your grandparents' (or great-grandparents') era. They had to bake the bread and cook the meat to make the sandwich. They probably had to walk to the grocery store to get the ingredients for lunch.

The other important side of this equation is what kind of nutrients are you getting for your calories? Treat calories as if they were money and spend them carefully. It is important to think about vitamins, minerals, and fiber as well as fat and calories. This may be a new concept for you. Most people have never thought about calories or food choices in this way. Think of the foods that are the "best buy" for you. Do you want a large serving of a low-calorie food, or

Count Calories Like Money

will you be satisfied with a very small portion of something high in calories? If you have 1,500 calories to "spend" in a day, are you willing to "spend" 500 of them on a dessert or 1,000 on a fast-food meal? Or does it make more sense to "budget" and distribute your calories over the whole day?

Modifying Recipes

How can you cut down on fat and calories without sacrificing taste? Is it possible to lose weight and still enjoy food?

Definitely!! Use the same techniques in your own kitchen that professional chefs use to modify recipes. Let's listen in on Pete, the chef we introduced in the first chapter as he talks to me, his dietitian. The examples that follow will give you ideas about how to modify your own favorite recipes.

Even though Chef Pete had taken nutrition classes for work he had never given a lot of thought to the amount of fat he ate until I asked him how much fat he used in food preparation at home. How many times did he add fat from force of habit, rather than necessity? How could he change some cooking strategies to use less fat? I asked Pete to think of a recipe for a favorite dish that he liked to prepare at home. He immediately replied veal scallopini. He lightly floured his veal cutlets and sautéed them in butter. He used about half of a stick of butter for two servings. I explained that half a stick of butter was 4 tablespoons or about 480 calories' worth of butter. I suggested that the next time Pete prepared veal scallopini he start with a quarter stick of butter or 2 tablespoons. If he used a nonstick skillet he may find that two tablespoons is enough to sauté the veal. If so, he would "save" 240 calories without radically changing what he was eating. I explained that if Pete could cut down just 250 calories a day and at the same time increase his physical activity expenditure by 250 calories a day he could burn 500 calories a day or 3,500 calories a week. Thirty-five hundred calories is equal to a pound.

Pete, like most people, thought he could do much better than that. I cautioned him that the important thing for him to do was to change his eating habits and increase his regular activity levels. I wanted Pete to make small changes he could maintain over time. When he said one pound a week was not enough, I reminded him that if he could lose one pound a week he would lose 52 pounds in a year, and he only needed to lose about 35 pounds. I encouraged him to concentrate on changing behavior rather than the numbers on the scale. I was concerned that he make healthful choices that could be maintained for the long run.

I suggested that Pete begin to modify some of his favorite recipes. I told Pete that if he faxed the modified recipes to me I would analyze them with my computer program and then we could discuss them at his next visit.

Pete faxed me a recipe for coq au vin, which is chicken cooked in wine. He had modified the original recipe by using boneless, skinless chicken breast halves instead of chicken parts with skin. This change meant that the serving size of chicken was smaller; however, it still provided a more than adequate amount of protein. He also cut out half of the amount of fat he added to the recipe. According to the computer analysis he saved about 200 calories per serving of chicken.

This modified recipe makes an elegant meal for company or a special occasion. This is a great recipe for company because you can do most of the work before your guests arrive and just pop the casserole into the oven and let it take care of itself for the last 30 to 40 minutes of cooking time. The rice and vegetable can be cooked on top of the stove or in the microwave after the chicken is in the oven. You can add a salad, dressing, and bread if you wish. It depends on how many calories you are allowing yourself at this particular meal.

Nutrition information is given for each recipe so you can make informed choices. The exchanges listed refer to the *Exchange List for Meal Planning*, a system developed by the American Diabetes Association and the American Dietetic Association to help people with diabetes make food choices. Instead of counting calories, you keep track of food you eat by categories referred to as *exchanges*. The concept will be more fully disclosed in chapter 6.

Pete's Coq au Vin

Servings: 4

INGREDIENTS

1 Tbsp. oil

4 boneless, skinless chicken breast halves (1 lb. raw)

½ tsp. salt

⅛ tsp. pepper

½ pound small white onions

½ pound mushrooms

½ cup sliced scallions

1 clove garlic, minced

2 Tbsp. flour

2 cups red wine

3 parsley sprigs

1 small bay leaf

⅛ tsp. dried thyme

snipped parsley

Put oil into a pan and heat. Brown chicken until golden on all sides. Sprinkle with salt and pepper, add onions and mushrooms. Simmer 15 minutes or until onions are partly tender and golden.

Preheat oven to 400° F.

Add scallions and garlic to the pan; simmer for two minutes. Stir in flour and then red wine. Cook, stirring until thickened. If the pan you have used for cooking to this point has handles that cannot go into the oven, transfer mixture to an ovenproof casserole. Add parsley sprigs, bay leaf, and thyme.

Bake chicken, covered, 30 to 40 minutes or until fork tender. Sprinkle casserole with snipped parsley. Serve over steamed rice. Add a green vegetable like broccoli, green beans, or asparagus for a complete meal.

NUTRITION FACTS

Nutrition information is for ¼ of the coq au vin. Rice and vegetable are additional.

Serving size: ¼ of recipe
Lean-meat exchanges: 4
Fat exchanges: 1
Starch exchanges: 1
Calories: 252   Calories from fat: 54
Total fat: 6 grams
Saturated fat: 1 gram

Cholesterol: 57 milligrams
Sodium: 374 milligrams
Carbohydrate: 17 grams
Dietary fiber: 2 grams
Sugars: 5 grams

Protein: 28 grams

Pete also faxed a recipe for stuffed zucchini squash. It was his favorite vegetable. In reality it is enough to be the major portion of a meal. This recipe contains cheese, eggs, bread crumbs, and milk as well as the vegetable. The stuffed zucchini was a recipe for a combination food, not merely a vegetable. It incorporated ingredients found on different levels of the food pyramid. In this recipe Pete cut down on the amount of cheese and totally eliminated the margarine. He used very sharp cheddar cheese because it is more flavorful. The very sharp cheddar cheese has the same number of calories and grams of fat as the mild variety. But its more intense flavor makes a smaller quantity of the sharp cheese as satisfying as the larger amount of the mild cheese. With these changes he saved about 90 calories per serving of stuffed zucchini. I suggested that Pete serve pasta with marinara sauce with the stuffed zucchini for a complete meatless meal.

You can prepare this dish ahead of time and refrigerate it until you are ready to bake it. The preparation time is about thirty minutes. It is much easier to remove the squashes from the shells if you let the squash cool first. That way you can handle the squash without burning your fingers.

If you wish, you can use a cholesterol-free egg substitute in the following recipes. That change will lower fat, cholesterol, and calories without changing taste.

_____ Stuffed Zucchini Squash _____

Servings: 4

INGREDIENTS

2 medium-size zucchini squashes
1½ cups fresh bread crumbs
  (2 slices of bread)
½ cup grated very sharp
  cheddar cheese (2 ounces)
¼ cup minced onion
2 Tbsp. minced parsley

½ tsp. salt
⅛ tsp. pepper
1 egg, beaten
¼ cup 1% milk

Scrub zucchini well under running water. Cut off ends, but do not peel. Cook whole with ¼ teaspoon salt in boiling water, about 5 to 6 minutes.

Preheat oven to 350° F.

Cool squashes. Cut squashes into halves, lengthwise. Using the tip of a teaspoon or a grapefruit spoon, carefully remove the center of the squash from the outer skin. Chop the pulp from the center of the squashes into small pieces and place into mixing bowl. Make soft bread crumbs, using the plastic blade on your food processor. Grate cheese and add bread crumbs and cheese to the squash pulp. Add remaining ingredients and mix thoroughly. Prepare an ovenproof pan by spraying with a nonstick cooking spray or wiping with a little oil on a paper towel. Place zucchini shells into shallow baking pan. Pile mixture into shells, making sure it is evenly divided. Bake uncovered for 30 minutes or until brown on top. Remove from oven and let sit about 10 minutes prior to serving.

NUTRITION FACTS

Serving size: ¼ of recipe
  (½ zucchini)
Starch exchanges: 1
Medium-fat meat exchanges: 1
Fat exchanges: 1
Calories: 195   Calories from
  fat: 89
Total fat: 10 grams
Saturated fat: 6 grams

Cholesterol: 79 milligrams
Sodium: 528 milligrams
Carbohydrate: 11 grams
Dietary fiber: 1 gram
Sugars: 4 grams
Protein: 9 grams

Chef Pete had also sent a recipe for apple muffins. In this recipe he substituted applesauce for the oil and used 2 percent instead of whole milk. Using applesauce in place of oil works well in quick breads and muffins. It is important to keep cooled muffins in an airtight container. Low-fat baked products tend to dry out more quickly than their full-fat counterparts.

Apple Muffins

Yield: 12 muffins

INGREDIENTS

1½ cups sifted all-purpose flour
½ tsp. cinnamon
2 tsp. double-acting
  baking powder
½ tsp. salt
½ cup sugar

1 egg
1 cup 2% milk
¼ cup applesauce
1 cup grated raw apple with
  skin (remove core first)

Preheat oven to 400° F.

Line a muffin tin with paper baking cups. Sift flour, cinnamon, baking powder, salt, and sugar into larger bowl. In a separate smaller bowl beat egg until frothy. Stir in milk, applesauce, and grated apple. Make a well in flour mixture. Pour liquid ingredients into dry ingredients all at once. Stir quickly, just until mixed. Do not beat. Mixture will be lumpy.

Fill muffin cups two-thirds full. Bake 25 minutes or until toothpick inserted into the center of a muffin comes out clean.

Remove muffins from tin immediately.

NUTRITION FACTS

Serving size: 1 muffin
Starch exchanges: 1½
Calories: 119   Calories from fat: 9
Total fat: 1 gram
Saturated fat: 0 grams
Cholesterol: 19 milligrams

Sodium: 180 milligrams
Carbohydrate: 25 grams
Dietary fiber: 2 grams
Sugars: 12 grams
Protein: 3 grams

In the muffin recipe Pete saved 40 calories per muffin.

When Pete returned to my office we discussed the recipes that he had modified. Pete was astounded to learn that the stuffed zucchini he had always considered a vegetable was a combination dish and the basis of a complete meal. He was learning about portion control. He could eat the foods he liked, but he needed to watch the amount of those foods. I encouraged him to eat slowly and savor his food. That way he would honestly be very satisfied with one reasonable-size portion. He was beginning to see what I meant about behavior changes. It was becoming apparent to him that if he wanted to lose weight and maintain that weight loss he would have to take a close look at behavior modification and portion control.

I encouraged Pete to continue modifying recipes. I said he could always question and analyze the amount of fat he put in food. He should ask himself what was it adding to the dish and would it be just as good with less or no added fat. I told Pete that if he did this regularly, pretty soon it would become second nature.

Pete said that his sessions with me had a side benefit. They were helping him with the "spa" menu at work. Public demand for good-tasting lower-calorie food is increasing, and the hotel and casino where Pete worked was responding to this demand.

There are lots of good-tasting lower-calorie foods available in restaurants and the grocery store these days. So why aren't we all thin? Chapter 5 will provide some answers and some surprises.

Watch Out for Portion Sizes

We live in a giant, economy-size world where we have all been conditioned from a very early age to think that more is better. Economy-size packaging has caught on everywhere from the supermarket to the convenience store. Consumers expect large portions and feel they are not getting their money's worth unless they get the largest size for the lowest price. While this is good for your pocketbook, it is a disaster for those of us who are trying to watch what we eat. One of the problems that arises when we buy the family-size package and there is only one of us is that we have to choose between waste or waist! Remember, just having food in the house tends to influence you to eat more than you need rather than have it go to waste or get stale. We have succumbed to the Big Gulp mentality, and we let our portion-size selection be determined by Madison Avenue advertisers rather than by common sense and good health. The evolution of large-size packaging parallels the obesity epidemic in the United

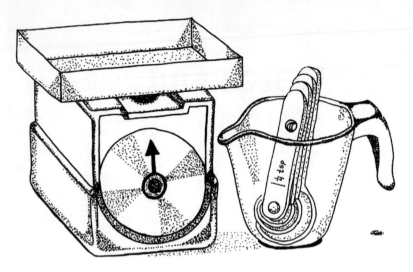

Weigh and Measure

States. Health smart consumers try to purchase the right quantity as well as a good quality of food.

In the "old" days a typical serving of a beverage was 6 or 8 ounces, yet today a Big Gulp, 64 ounces, is the norm. Sixty-four ounces is two quarts. But, you say, it lasts all morning or all afternoon. Nonetheless, most times the beverage (and yes, I do know that some of it is ice) is high in calories and low in other nutrients. Convenience stores and food courts feature large paper cups for beverages, and the fountain dispensers serve "empty calorie" choices.

And it is not just packaging. The glasses, cups, plates, and bowls we use every day are larger than they used to be. I recently found a catalog dated 1947 describing china and glassware. It talked about "everyday" glasses in three sizes: 4 ounce, 8 ounce, and 12 ounce. All of the different sets of glasses came in the same standard sizes regardless of the color or style of the glasses. A current catalog describing sets of casual glassware listed thirteen different sizes of glasses ranging from 10 to 21 ounces. The U.S. Department of Agriculture (USDA) nutrition experts have determined that a serving of juice is 4 ounces and a serving of milk is 8 ounces, and in 1947 the serving size matched the size of glasses commonly available. That is no longer true today. While the size of the glassware has changed, the size of the portion we *should* consume has not. Dinner plates all used to be ten inches in diameter. Now they come in a variety of sizes starting at ten inches. Soup and cereal bowls were a standard 8 ounces. I recently saw some 16-ounce cereal bowls advertised. No matter how conscientiously you try to eat the right size portion, it is difficult to accurately judge amounts when using different size glasses, plates, cups, and bowls unless you take the time to measure.

A 1938 cookbook offers advice on how to shop for a family. The author recommends purchasing no more than ¼ pound of meat per adult per day. It also advises that "flesh" (meat, fish, and poultry) should not be eaten more than once a day. It is important to remember that ¼ pound of raw meat with no bone will shrink when cooked to approximately 3 ounces. A current cookbook uses ½ pound as a standard serving and makes no recommendations about the quantity to eat each day. How times have changed! If you intend to take control of your diabetes and your overall health, it is important to control what you eat. *Portion size is just as important as basic food choices if you want to be healthy and maintain good glucose control.*

Some restaurants now feature 16-ounce steaks—one whole pound—and portions of prime rib that start at 12 ounces, and typical hamburgers contain a half pound of ground meat. On the other hand, the USDA says a serving of meat is a three-ounce cooked portion. The USDA is the government agency that originally analyzed food to determine its caloric and nutrient content. They began over 100 years ago and published the first tables of food composition in 1896. The American Diabetes Association and the American Dietetic Association's *Exchange Lists for Meal Planning* is based on the USDA data base, as are all the reputable computer nutrient analysis programs. Most popular diet books that give the number of calories for foods also use the "official" size serving. Most Americans eat large portions, and if they are counting, they almost always underestimate the quantity they have eaten.

If you do not know the quantity of food you are eating you will have a very difficult time trying to control your blood glucose. Do you have a glass of juice for breakfast? How many ounces or how many servings of juice does the glass hold?

Tomorrow morning, when you pour your glass, try this experiment. Before you take that first sip, pour the juice into a measuring cup to see how much you have. Four ounces or ½ cup of apple, grapefruit, orange, and pineapple juice and just ⅓ of a cup grape and prune juice, count as a 60-calorie serving. If you drink a whole cup, or 8 ounces of juice, you are drinking two or three servings of fruit rather than one. In reality, you are drinking a 120- or 180-calorie glass of juice, when in your mind you might think that you had consumed a 60-calorie glass of juice. Do the same thing with your cereal and see how it compares to the serving you think you are eating.

I know this may be inconvenient, but if you really want to know the amount of food you eat you have to weigh or measure it. There are some shortcuts to make it easier for you. For example, if you drink fruit juice at home you need to figure out how much is the right amount to drink. Pour 4 ounces of juice into a glass measuring cup. Then pour the juice into the type of glass you would normally use to serve the juice. Then look to see if there is any mark or design on the glass that you can use as an informal way to measure the 4 ounces of juice. For example, if 4 ounces of juice comes to the second line on the glass then all you have to do in the future is to pour the juice to the second line and you will have your 4-ounce portion. As long as you use the same glasses for juice you will never have to use a measuring cup to measure your 4 ounces of juice. If your glass does not have a convenient marking, then you could wrap your hand around the glass and use your fingers to measure how much juice to pour. The key is to find an easy way to determine the amount of juice or other beverage you want to drink.

You can do the same thing with your cereal. Measure the amount you should eat and then put it in your bowl. Is there a marking on the bowl that you can use to see if you have the right amount of cereal? If so, your measuring has become easy. Another way you can do this if you do not wish to measure at every meal is by measuring the quantity of food your serving utensils hold. If you use the same serving spoons, scoops and ladles regularly, measure how much they hold so you will know how much you are getting at each meal.

You can also use the weight on the package to get a good idea of your portion. If you buy a package of boneless, skinless chicken breasts that weighs one pound you know that it is 16 ounces. Sixteen ounces of raw meat will shrink approximately 25 percent when you cook it and give you 12 ounces of cooked chicken. If you are serving a 3-ounce portion then you know that one quarter of those 12 ounces of cooked chicken is the desired amount to serve each person and that you have enough for 4 servings in a one-pound package of raw chicken.

If you are really serious about blood glucose and/or weight control you should purchase and use a kitchen scale.

Kitchen scales come in a wide variety of styles and price ranges. If you like gadgets and want to spend the money, you can get digital scales that will accurately weigh to a fraction of an ounce or to grams. Some of these scales will tell you the number of calories in the amount of different foods you are weighing. But you do not need a scale with all these features. You can find good portion scales that are much more economical. Scales are available in the housewares department of any department or hardware store. You may also be able to find them in large drugstores or supermarkets.

Once you have invested in the scale, be sure to get your money's worth by using it to make sure you eat the correct portion of food. Remember to weigh and measure foods in the ready-to-eat state. Some foods, like meat, fish, and poultry, shrink when they are cooked, so if you weigh your portion in the raw state you will actually be eating less than you thought. On the other hand, some foods like rice, pasta, and hot cereals expand when you cook them. For example, rice will triple in volume when you cook it. One cup of raw rice will produce three cups or six servings of cooked rice.

Knowing how cooking affects the volume of food can help you determine the amount to cook in the first place. If you cook and serve the appropriate amount of food you will be much less likely to overeat. If you are cooking for two and serving rice for dinner and wish to serve one-half cup to each person, start with one-third cup of raw rice. Remember that rice will triple in volume when cooked. So one-third cup raw rice will give you one cup or two one-half cup servings of cooked rice.

If you are sure you will always be hungry if you start to measure and eat smaller portions, start by weighing a typical portion of meat you normally eat. If it weighs 12 ounces you could begin to modify your portion size by cutting down to a 10-ounce cooked portion. If you cut down gradually you will become accustomed to the smaller portion and soon be just as satisfied with 10 ounces as you currently are with 12 ounces. You can continue to cut down, a little at a time, until you reach your blood glucose and weight goals. If you are trying to cut down on your portions of meat, try eating some raw vegetables such as carrots or celery as an appetizer and that will help fill you up. Your body will adjust to less meat and you will soon find yourself full after eating a smaller quantity. You may be skeptical, but you will never know if this technique will work unless you give it a chance.

There are a lot of common household items that you can use to estimate serving size, and learning how to do this would be especially useful when eating away from home. A deck of cards is a time-honored comparison for three ounces of cooked meat, and if you are looking at a beef patty, three ounces will be about the same size as the top of a mayonnaise jar. A serving of grapes (about seventeen grapes) will fit nicely into the palm of your hand (if you are a woman or a man with a small hand). A medium-size piece of fresh fruit is the same size as a tennis ball and a tablespoon of mayonnaise is about the size of a quarter.

Many people do not pay any attention to how much fruit they eat. They mistakenly think because it is "natural" they can have as much as they want. If you believe this, the next time you decide to eat a quarter of a watermelon check your blood glucose first and then again thirty minutes later. You will learn that it is a better choice to have a smaller portion of the watermelon. Seeing for yourself how food and portion size affect your blood glucose will help you to make better choices.

Try to incorporate some of the things you have learned about portion size into making meals at home. I will use the following recipe for spaghetti with meat sauce to illustrate exactly how important portion size can be.

——————— Spaghetti Sauce ———————

Servings: 8

INGREDIENTS

1 pound extralean ground beef	30 ounces water
1 small onion, minced	1 tsp. Italian herbs
1 clove garlic, minced	½ tsp. oregano
3 8-ounce cans tomato sauce	½ tsp. pepper
1 6-ounce can tomato paste	

Place meat, onion, and garlic in a heavy pan deep enough to hold all the ingredients. Turn the heat on low, to brown ingredients without adding any additional fat, as there is plenty in the ground beef. Using a large fork or spatula, stir to break up the meat so it will be evenly distributed throughout the sauce. When onion turns translucent and meat begins to brown, add the rest of the ingredients and cook about three hours over very low heat, until sauce is thick.

Makes about six cups of sauce; eight ¾-cup servings. Serve over cooked pasta.

NUTRITION FACTS
(FIGURES DO NOT INCLUDE PASTA)

Serving size: ⅛ of recipe, about ¾ of a cup
Starch exchanges: 1
Medium-fat meat exchanges: 2
Calories: 200   Calories from fat: 108

Sodium: 612 milligrams (If you want a lower sodium version use no added salt or reduced-sodium tomato sauce.)
Carbohydrate: 12 grams

Total fat: 12 grams   Dietary fiber: 2 grams
Saturated fat: 5 grams   Sugars: 4 grams
Cholesterol: 43 milligrams   Protein: 12 grams

To cook pasta, follow the directions on the package, then drain well in a colander or strainer. Place pasta on plate and top with sauce. If you wish, you can add the drained pasta to the sauce and mix it before serving.

This recipe makes 8 servings. If you live alone or there are only two people in your household, you can easily freeze the extra sauce for future meals. Portion the sauce into plastic containers with tight-fitting lids. Put just enough sauce for a meal into each container. Then you will have just the amount you need when you thaw it.

If you divide this into 4 servings, each serving would be about one cup of pasta and 1½ cups of sauce and have about 570 calories. If you follow the *Exchange Lists for Meal Planning* this amount of pasta and meat sauce would equal 4 medium-fat meat choices and 4½ carbohydrate choices. If you divide the same amount into 6 servings each one would be ¾ cup of pasta and one cup of sauce and about 400 calories or 3 medium-fat meat and 3 carbohydrate choices. If you make 8 servings out of the same pasta and sauce, each serving would be ½ cup of pasta and ¾ cup of sauce and be about 285 calories or 2 medium-fat meat choices and 2 carbohydrate choices. What you are learning is how important it is to make choices, as you are the only person who can determine the quantity of food you eat.

You will find that it is much easier to control your portions if you prepare the appropriate quantity of food for each meal. Freeze foods like the spaghetti sauce in meal-size amounts, so you will have only the predetermined amount you want to eat for a meal. This is an efficient way to handle any food, especially if you prepare meals for one or two people. This approach works well for soups, stews, chili, or other foods that are typically prepared in family-size batches. For people who live alone and want to limit a serving of spaghetti sauce to one cup, the easy solution is to freeze it in one-cup-size containers.

How much pasta should you cook for each serving? The rule of thumb is that pasta doubles when cooked. Two ounces of dry pasta is about ½ cup and when cooked will double to 1 cup. The problem with pasta is that its shape makes it difficult to measure ½ or ¼ cup dry; however, ¼ cup of dry pasta weighs 1 ounce. It is much easier to weigh the pasta before you cook it and that way you know that you are getting the exact amount you want to eat. One ounce of dry pasta will be ½ cup when it is cooked, just the right amount for a serving.

You will discover that the pasta manufacturers and the Food and Drug Administration (they regulate food labels) have deemed that ½ cup or 2 ounces of dry pasta is a serving and contains 210 calories, but you know that is 1 cup cooked. The more you practice this the more you will realize how important it is that you take charge of your own portion sizes if you want to be in charge of your blood glucose, your weight, and your health.

Sam, the older gentleman we met in the first chapter, was a retired engineer and used the skills he developed over a lifetime in his chosen profession to help manage his diabetes. He had always prided himself on getting good value for his hard-earned dollar. When grocery shopping became his responsibility, he looked for bargains and frequently purchased the large economy-size package to get the lowest unit price. It wasn't long until Sam called me complaining of boredom with eating the same food all the time. I pointed out that Sam had fallen victim to the large economy "bargain"-size syndrome. I suggested he try smaller packages of individual foods so that he could incorporate more variety.

Sam tried this with meat. Actually, he went a bit further. He bought a food scale and used it with great regularity to ensure that he was eating the right size portions. Whenever he purchased meat he weighed portion size servings and packaged them individually for freezing; that way he had the right amount for a meal in each package. He weighed his pasta and rice prior to cooking and that way did not have to deal with figuring out what to do with leftovers or be tempted to overeat because the food was cooked and *ready*. On his grocery shopping lists he started to indicate not only the items he wanted to purchase but the amount of food as well. As a result, his pantry and freezer were stocked with a wide variety of foods that he liked to eat and he was saving money because he was buying the right quantity for his needs.

Portion size is important for blood glucose control, but what about sugar and carbohydrates? Chapter 6 gives you the facts about these nutrients.

Sugar and Carbohydrates: Not Forbidden Foods

I n ancient times diabetes mellitus was diagnosed by the sweet taste of urine in patients with diabetes. For years even the medical community called it "sugar diabetes." The question of sugar in the diet of people with diabetes was first addressed in 1550 B.C. Physicians, in the days before insulin was discovered, thought that people who lost sugar in their urine needed to replace it in their diet. Meal plans were made up of foods like grains, grapes, honey, and sweet beer. The optimal amount of sugar and carbohydrate in the diet has been a topic of clinical discussion and scientific research for thousands of years. Today we know that we need to be concerned about total carbohydrate and good nutrition, not just sugar.

Some of the confusion about eating foods with sugar arises from the fact that when most people think about sugar they think of table sugar. The chemical name for table sugar is sucrose. Raw sugar, brown sugar, and confectioner's sugar are also sucrose. They are all digested and absorbed by the body the same way. But sucrose is only one kind of sugar. Fructose, lactose, and maltose are other sugars found in food. All of these "sugars" break down to glucose in the body. Carbohydrate or starch also breaks down to glucose in the body.

For years, medical professionals believed that there was a direct relationship between the amount of table sugar (sucrose) consumed and the level of glucose in the blood. They also believed that since "complex" carbohydrate was a bigger molecule than sucrose, it would take longer for it to turn to sugar (glucose) than for sucrose to turn to glucose in the blood. It only made sense. But modern research has turned all of this upside down and decisions can now be made based on the most current information.

In 1994 the American Diabetes Association Nutrition Recommendations for Persons with Diabetes stated that sucrose restriction in the diet for diabetes cannot be justified on the basis of its glycemic effect. (The effect that sugar has on blood glucose.) Studies show that many starchy foods—for example, white bread or corn flakes—produce a greater rise in blood glucose than table sugar (sucrose). Research also shows that other sweeteners such as honey, molasses, corn syrup, and fruit juice affect the blood glucose in the same way that sucrose does. In other words they are no better or worse than table sugar. Dietary fructose does affect blood glucose more slowly; however "high fructose corn syrup" contains a good deal of glucose in addition to the fructose.

When making any decisions about how much or what kind of sugar to include in your meal plan, you need to think about how that sugar will affect your blood glucose control. But it is also important to keep in mind what part sugar plays in overall healthy food choices. Sugars and starches may affect your blood glucose in a similar manner, but that is not the only thing to think about when making food choices. Many carbohydrate foods are good sources of vitamins, minerals, and dietary fiber, while most natural sweeteners—for example, table sugar, honey, or maple syrup—contribute primarily calories. Don't look only at sugar but at total carbohydrate and the effect it has on your blood glucose.

There are a lot of things to think about when making choices about which sweetener to use. Is the sweetener artificial or natural? Is it low-calorie or not? Most important, how does the sweetener fit into an overall healthful diet? Everyone has a certain number of calories to spend in a day. Your age, height, activity level, and gender determine that number. No matter how many calories you have to spend in a day, think of them as if they were your money and spend them just as carefully. If, for example, you wanted to drink a carbonated beverage, you could choose a regular or a diet drink. If you choose 12 ounces of Diet Coke you will drink zero calories, and zero carbohydrate. If you select 12 ounces of Coca-Cola Classic you will drink 140 calories and 39 grams of carbohydrate. Neither beverage is a source of vitamins, protein, or fiber. You are the only person who can decide if the Coca-Cola Classic is worth the 140 calories.

Let me tell you about a child who we will call Mark who developed diabetes when he was five years old. Mark's dad was a dentist and he had two older sisters. One of the first questions Mark's mom asked me was how many diet sodas Mark could drink each day. I responded that Mark could drink the same number of diet sodas as he had regular sodas before his diabetes had been diagnosed. Mark's mom made the same mistake most people make when it comes to sugar and diabetes. Instead of asking what is an appropriate or healthful amount of sugar to eat, the typical response is

"How much can I have?" A better question to ask is: "After I have eaten a healthful selection of grains, vegetables, fruits, and lean protein, how many calories do I have left to spend on calorie-dense rather than nutrient-dense foods?" It is important to keep in mind that if you want something sweet it should be part of your overall selection for the day and or meal. Though one carbohydrate can be substituted for another, if sugar is added rather than substituted for other carbohydrates there will be a problem. Remember, your ultimate goal is to control your blood glucose.

Whether we like to think about it or not, the old adage "you are what you eat" really is true. All people, not just those with diabetes, need to make good food choices in order to be healthy. Nevertheless, sugar is the one nutrient we think of when we hear diabetes.

Our daily food choices have an impact on the development of a number of chronic diseases such as heart disease, elevated cholesterol, high blood pressure and some cancers as well as diabetes. From a practical standpoint foods that have traditionally been considered forbidden for people with diabetes are the same foods people concerned with other chronic diseases should also consume in moderation.

Over the years, diabetes educators have worked to help people with diabetes understand these complicated concepts. The *Exchange Lists for Meal Planning* booklet has been developed by the American Diabetes and American Dietetic Associations to help teach people with diabetes consistent eating habits. The booklet lists foods in categories according to carbohydrate, protein, and fat content. Foods with similar nutrient content are put on a list. The "ready to eat" serving size of the food is given as well. The foods are listed either by the food's name or major nutrient. The *Exchange Lists* can be very helpful when deciding how much of a sweet food to eat. Because carbohydrates turn to glucose in the body, eating the same amount of carbohydrate every day at meals and snacks can help you keep your blood glucose and your diabetes in good control.

The *Exchange Lists* classify foods into the following categories.

Goups/lists:	Carbohydrate (grams)	Protein (grams)	Fat (grams)	Calories
Carbohydrate Group				
Starch	15	3	1 or less	80
Fruit	15	—	—	60
Milk				
Skim or 1%	12	8	0–3	90
Low-fat or 2%	12	8	5	120
Whole	12	8	8	150
Other carbohydrates	15	varies	varies	varies
Vegetables	5	2	—	25
Meat and Meat Substitute Group				
Very lean	—	7	0–1	35
Lean	—	7	3	55
Medium-fat	—	7	5	75
High-fat	—	7	8	100
Fat Group	—	—	5	45

As you can see, carbohydrate and protein amounts are similar in different foods, but the big variation is in the fat and calories. Let's use milk as an example. All milk has 12 grams of carbohydrate and 8 grams of protein; only the fat and calories vary. If you look at the label on milk containers you will see that all of the carbohydrate is sugar. All the carbohydrate in the milk comes from lactose or milk sugar. If you eat 12 grams of carbohydrate in the form of table sugar as part of a meal instead of drinking milk, it would have an equivalent affect on your blood glucose as the milk; however, you would not get the protein, calcium, riboflavin, and other nutrients the milk contains.

Exchanges

The amount of the food you eat is very important. While you can exchange one food for another, you need to select the amount of food listed as one serving. For example 12 sweet, fresh cherries are equivalent in carbohydrate to 17 small grapes. This gets to the heart of the matter. When was the last time you counted the number of cherries or grapes you ate? Most of us never do.

The table on the following page includes some common favorite desserts and snacks. The reason fat is included is that frequently foods that are high in carbohydrate and sucrose are also high in fat. For example, chocolate candy can have more calories from fat than it does from sugar. Nevertheless most people classify chocolate candy as a sweet food, rather than a fat food.

Look at the foods listed in the table of foods commonly eaten and think about which foods you enjoy eating and which foods are the most satisfying. Most of the foods are listed in 15-gram carbohydrate portions because that is the recommended serving size. If you use the food lists in the *Exchange* booklet you will see that all foods are listed in 15-gram carbohydrate portion size. If you want to obtain a copy of the *Exchange Lists for Meal Planning* call your local office of the American Diabetes Association or 1–800–342–2383.

Comparison of Foods Commonly Eaten

Food/Portion	Carbohydrate (grams)	Fat (grams)	Protein (grams)	Calories
1 small scoop vanilla ice cream ($\frac{1}{2}$ cup)	15	10	—	150
1 slice apple pie ($\frac{1}{8}$ of pie)	43	14	2	306
1 miniature Hershey's bar	5	3	—	47
1 cup fresh raspberries	15	—	—	60
1 ounce potato chips	15	10	2	152
1 ounce pretzels	22	1.5	1	114
1 ounce popcorn, plain (3 cups)	22	1.5	1	114
$\frac{1}{2}$ cup Jell-O, any flavor	19	—	—	80
8 ounces 1% milk	12	1–3	10	100
1 Tbsp. pancake syrup	15	—	—	60
2 pancakes, 4-in. diameter	15	6	3	126
$\frac{1}{2}$ cup mashed potato	15	0–1	3	80
1 slice bread (1 oz.)	15	0–1	3	80
1 corn tortilla, 6-in. diameter (no fat)	15	0–1	3	80
1 taco shell, 6-in. diameter	15	6	3	125
$\frac{1}{2}$ cup orange juice	15	—	—	60
$\frac{1}{3}$ cup grape juice	15	—	—	60
1 orange, small	15	—	—	60
17 grapes, small	15	—	—	60
1 kiwi	15	—	—	60
$\frac{1}{2}$ cup applesauce, unsweetened	15	—	—	60

Portion size is important. If you look at the table of common foods you see that two pancakes 4 inches in diameter is a serving (15 grams of carbohydrate). Adding 1 tablespoon of syrup to those pancakes adds another serving (15 grams of carbohydrate). The problem of course is that 1 tablespoon of syrup does not cover the two pancakes. So you must make a choice. You can simply eat more syrup and watch your blood glucose skyrocket, or you can choose another topping for your pancakes such as the ½ cup of applesauce or 1 cup of fresh raspberries. If you really want to have the pancake syrup, you need to substitute it for some other carbohydrate in that meal. That may mean eating the syrup in place of fruit or milk. You can do that once in a while, but if you make a habit of it you will not get the vitamins, minerals, and fiber that you need for a healthful diet, as syrup adds calories but few other nutrients.

The Pie or the Sandwich?

If you wish to eat a 15-gram carbohydrate portion of the apple pie you would need to cut it into three and eat only one third of the piece of pie. What about the ice cream that everyone knows rightfully belongs on top of the pie? If you eat the whole piece of pie with the ice cream you would get 58 grams of carbohydrate at one time. It would be the carbohydrate equivalent of eating a sandwich with two slices of whole-grain bread, an 8-ounce glass of milk, and a small orange. The biggest difference is in the fat column. The pie and ice cream contain 24 grams of fat and 446 calories. The sandwich lunch of two slices of bread, 8 ounces of 1 percent milk, and a small orange contains less than 5 grams of fat and 320 calories.

	Apple Pie à la Mode	Sandwich Lunch
Carbohydrate	58 grams	57 grams
Fat	24 grams	4.4 grams
Calories	446	320
Vitamin A	37.50 Re	171.5 RE
Vitamin C	4 mg.	72 mg.
Folate	5 ug.	83 ug.
Calcium	73 mg.	447 mg.
Sodium	362 mg.	420 mg.
Fiber	2.1 grams	5.8 grams

It is pretty easy to see which choice offers the most nutrients. Select the meat of your choice to put on that sandwich. It will add protein, fat, and calories. However, meat does not contain carbohydrate, so the two ounces you would put on the sandwich will have very little effect on your blood glucose.

You have to keep in mind that when you eat a sandwich, a glass of milk, and a piece of fruit you have had a complete lunch. Most of us would eat pie and ice cream as dessert, not as a whole meal. So that 58 grams of carbohydrate from dessert would be added to whatever you may have eaten at that meal. All of these factors complicate the sugar issue. People who have diabetes must be concerned about how sugar and other sources of carbohydrate affect their blood glucose. Everyone, not just people with diabetes, should be concerned about how food choices affect their overall health. In the event that you control your diabetes with insulin, you can take extra insulin if you eat extra carbohydrate and keep your blood glucose in an acceptable range. However, if you are constantly fighting the battle of the bulge, you must be aware that any "extra" calories you eat will be stored in your body in the form of fat. This is true for everyone, whether they have diabetes or not. This is why we have been saying for years that a diabetic diet is a diet that is good for everyone.

Sugar Replacers

Sugar replacers fit into two broad categories: those that contain calories and those that do not. But calories are just one consideration. Other concerns revolve around safety. Calorie-free sugar substitutes are called artificial sweeteners. Just the term *artificial* raises a red flag to most people. These issues are not new. The controversy over the safety of artificial sweeteners dates back a century. Saccharin has been used for over 100 years in the United States and while it seems to have stood the test of time scientists still have not given it a clean bill of health. Every product containing saccharin sold in this country must be labeled with the warning: "Use of this product may be hazardous to your health. This product contains saccharin which has been shown to cause cancer in laboratory animals."

Despite the warning labels, many people who have diabetes find that foods and beverages containing these sugar replacers help make managing their diabetes a little bit easier. Currently there are 4 low-calorie sweeteners approved for use in the United States:

Saccharin is a white powder that is about 300 times sweeter than table sugar and is used mainly as a "tabletop" sweetener. It was discovered accidentally in 1879 and is made from petroleum. It is commonly sold as Sweet'n Low and is packaged with dextrose. Each serving contains ½ gram of carbohydrate. The warning label is based on research conducted on laboratory rats. There are no documented reports of any problems in humans. There is still controversy among the experts about whether or not it is safe for pregnant women.

Aspartame is a synthetic sweetener made from protein. It contains 4 calories per gram, and is 200 times sweeter than table sugar. Even though it contains the same number of calories per gram as sugar, you will use far less because it is so much sweeter. That is why it does not affect your blood glucose. Aspartame's discovery in 1965 was also an accident. It took until 1981 to hit the grocery store shelves. It is known as Equal when used as a "tabletop" sweetener and NutraSweet when it is used as an ingredient. Phenylalanine is one of the amino acids that make up this sweetener. People who have phenylketonuria, a genetic metabolic disorder diagnosed in infancy, should not use aspartame. People with this disease cannot metabolize this amino acid, and if they eat it they accumulate toxic waste in the body that causes brain damage. That is why all products that contain NutraSweet must list the warning "Phenylketonurics: contains phenylalanine." The FDA says this product is safe for the general population although they acknowledge that some people have an "unusual sensitivity" to aspartame.

Acesulfame K was discovered in Germany in 1967. It is 200 times sweeter than table sugar and is heat stable, which means you can use it in cooking. It combines well with other sweeteners and does not have any aftertaste. It is known as Sweet One or Swiss Sweet as a "tabletop" sweetener and Sunett as an ingredient. No safety concerns have been reported about this sweetener.

Sucralose is 600 times sweeter than table sugar and is made from table sugar that is chemically changed so your body does not absorb its calories. It is the newest sweetener on the market and is sold under the name of Splenda. No health risks have been reported for this sweetener.

An important **safety note** to remember about sweeteners is that any problem is usually dose related. That means that the more you consume the greater your odds of having a problem. The bottom line is to treat sweeteners like all foods and remember moderation and variety.

There are three other sweeteners that have been submitted to the FDA for approval in this country. **Alitame** is a protein-based sweetener that is 2,000 times as sweet as table sugar. It is used in Australia, China, Mexico, and New Zealand. **Cyclamate** is 30 times sweeter than table sugar and was in use in the United States from the 1950s until 1970. It was banned because of studies that showed it caused cancer in test animals; however, its safety for human use is supported by the research. It is marketed in over 50 countries throughout the world. If you travel outside the United States you may encounter these two sweeteners. The third sweetener that has been submitted to the FDA is **neotame**. It is protein based and is 30 times sweeter than aspartame. It is not being sold in any other countries.

Sugar Alcohols

Sugar alcohols are sweeteners that provide calories and have less impact on blood glucose than table sugar or other carbohydrates. Mannitol, sorbitol, and xylitol are common sugar alcohols found in foods that are marketed to people with diabetes. Isomalt, lactitol, and hydrogenated starch hydrolysates are newer sugar alcohols and were introduced into foods during the 1980s. These sugar alcohols may also be called polyols and are considered nutritive sweeteners because they do provide calories. They are not broken down in the mouth and consequently help prevent tooth decay and are an ingredient of sugarless gum.

Mannitol is not as sweet as table sugar and provides only 1.6 calories per gram. It is used as an ingredient in powdered foods and gum. It occurs naturally in some fruits and vegetables, for example asparagus, carrots, sweet potatoes, and pineapple.

Sorbitol is only about half as sweet as table sugar and provides 2.6 calories per gram. It is used as a sweetener in candies, gum, jams, and jellies. It occurs naturally in apples, berries, cherries, pears, plums, and prunes.

Xylitol is just about equal to table sugar in sweetness and provides 2.4 calories per gram. It is used as a sweetener and flavoring in toothpaste, mints, and gum. It occurs naturally in cauliflower, raspberries, and strawberries.

Isomalt is about half as sweet as table sugar and provides 2 calories per gram. Isomalt is used in candies, ice cream, baked goods, and gum. It does not occur naturally and is made from sucrose or table sugar.

Lactitol is less than half as sweet as sugar and provides 2 calories per gram. It is used in ice cream, candy, baked goods, and sugar substitutes. It does not occur naturally and is made from lactose or milk sugar.

Hydrogenated starch hydrolysates are just about as sweet as sugar and provide fewer than 3 calories per gram. They are used in candy, baked goods, and toothpaste. They do not occur naturally and are made from corn, potato, and wheat starches.

The last six sweeteners listed are all polyols. Eating foods containing polyols could cause diarrhea if too much is eaten at one time. Labels on sugar-free candy that contain polyols carry the warning: "Hydrogenated starch hydrolysate and sorbitol may cause a laxative effect in children and other sensitive individuals when this serving size is eaten in one sitting. We recommend starting with a smaller serving size of approximately 6 candies (15g)."

Make Informed Choices

Many people think that if a food is sugar-free then they can eat all they want. One woman I know did that with some candy and ended up with diarrhea that lasted two days. On top of the outcome she said the candy didn't even taste that good. It is important to remember that sugar-free foods need to be treated like any other food. Taste is the number one reason why people select specific foods. Do not waste or "spend" calories on food unless it really tastes good to you. Look to see how it fits into your overall meal plan for the day or week. Make informed choices. Look at the label information from two chocolate bars with almonds. One was made with sugar and one without.

	Hershey's Milk Chocolate with Almonds	Fifty 50 Almond Chocolate Bar (sugar-free)
Serving size	41 grams	43 grams
Calories	230	240
Total fat	14 grams	18 grams
Saturated fat	7 grams	10 grams
Carbohydrate	20 grams	17 grams
Sugars (part of total carb.)	18 grams	0 grams

From a practical standpoint, there is no real advantage in choosing foods made with sugar alcohols over foods made with other nutritive sweeteners. It is true that polyols are lower in calories than other carbohydrates; however, you need to compare the individual food items. The "regular" food may or may not be lower in calories than the sugar-free version. You also need to compare the taste and see which version will satisfy you. Sugar-free foods are not magic potions and eating them offers no guarantee you will keep your blood glucose under control. They do provide more food choices and can be helpful to some people. **The most important thing to remember is that sugar-free does not mean calorie-free.** Sugar-free products need to be incorporated into your overall meal plan just like any other food. Many products that contain sugar replacers have significant amounts of carbohydrate, fat, protein, and calories.

Many people who have diabetes are afraid to eat anything that contains sugar. What you really need to remember is that sugar is just like any other carbohydrate and the amount you can include in the foods you eat will be determined by its impact on your blood glucose. Sugar-free foods may have a place in your diet, but they are not "free" and need to be included as a part of an overall healthful meal plan.

Fat, like sugar and carbohydrate, is another important nutrient, and all fats are not the same. Chapter 7 discusses their differences and why you might want to select one type over another, or in some cases a fat substitute for fat.

Figuring Fat: Which Kinds and How Much to Eat

F*at* is a word that evokes an emotional response in many people. Most people do not want to be fat. Yet most of us like the taste of fat because it is one of the things that adds flavor to food. Many of us become obsessed about counting fat grams. What is fat, anyway? How many kinds are there? Why are we so concerned about fat, and does it really make any difference? This chapter will talk about what you need to know about fat and why you need to know it, and it will expose the hidden sources of fat and give you the facts needed to make wise food choices.

An important thing to keep in mind is that with modern technology fat is more readily available to eat than it was a hundred years ago. Your great-grandmother had to milk the cow and separate the cream and then churn the butter. Or slaughter the pig to get the lard to make the piecrust. She then had to pick the apples, wash, peel, and slice them to make the pie. Today, we walk into modern markets and have instant access to the hot bakery pie. Great-grandma burned a large portion of the calories from the pie with the effort it took to make it. We don't! Consequently, we must be very selective in choosing the fat we eat. We have to have some, but we don't want too much.

Who Needs Fat?

We all need fat. Fat is an essential nutrient, which means we can't live without it. Our body does not make all the components we need nutritionally, so we must get them from the food we eat. The fat we consume, like protein and carbohydrate, is an important source of energy for our bodies. Fat is the most concentrated source of energy, as it provides 9 calories in each gram. To put that in perspective, protein and carbohydrate each provide 4 calories per gram. (There are about 28 grams of weight in one ounce.)

The fat we eat plays an important role in keeping us healthy. First of all, it helps the body to use protein and carbohydrate efficiently. It supplies essential fatty acids, helps to maintain our skin, and is necessary for metabolism and regulation of body processes. Fat is a carrier of fat-soluble vitamins A, D, E, and K, and without fat your body cannot use these vitamins. Fat also plays an important role in insulating the body and in supporting and cushioning vital organs. It is also the storage source for energy. You have to eat a certain amount of fat, but if you eat too much or too little you will get into trouble.

How Much Fat Should We Eat?

The Dietary Guidelines for Americans were developed by experts at the United States Department of Agriculture

(USDA) and the U.S. Department of Health and Human Services (HHS) and are recommendations on healthful eating for all Americans. These governmental agencies convene meetings of experts from universities, hospitals and research institutions to determine what type of advice to give the public. The guidelines are the result of a consensus by scientific researchers and clinicians and give practical guidelines to the general public. The Dietary Guidelines recommend that Americans consume no more than 30 percent of their total calories as fat, with no more than 10 percent of total calories as saturated fat.

The American Diabetes Association (ADA) nutrition recommendations are based on the same science as the Dietary Guidelines. However, the ADA recommendations also look at the effect of food on your blood glucose. They emphasize that the amount and type of fat you eat should be based on your own individualized nutrition needs and goals, which should be determined by an assessment of your current status. If you have diabetes then your goals are to keep your cholesterol, triglycerides, and blood glucose all within acceptable ranges. For adults, a cholesterol level of less than 200 milligrams per deciliter (mg/dl), an LDL cholesterol (bad or harmful cholesterol) of less than 130 mg/dl, and triglycerides less than 200 mg/dl is considered acceptable by all the experts.

The amount and type of fat you eat as well as the amount of exercise you get may influence these numbers. Blood glucose control can also affect your lipids, which is yet another reason to keep your blood glucose in the normal range. Some people may require medication in addition to diet and exercise to control their blood lipids. It is important to remember that medication be given in addition to, not as a replacement for, diet and exercise.

How Many Kinds of Fat Are There?

The first thing you need to know is that we are talking about "fats" in the plural sense, as there is no one type of "fat" found in food. Fats are made of chemical compounds that contain fatty acids. The three main fatty acids found in food are **saturated**, **monounsaturated**, and **polyunsaturated**. All fats are made up of three elements that are commonly found in nature. These elements are oxygen, hydrogen and carbon atoms. Fats contain mostly hydrogen and carbon and relatively little oxygen. That is what makes them very "fuel efficient" nutrients.

You may be wondering what foods contain which kind of fat. What foods are good or bad and what foods should you avoid? All foods and all types of fat can be included in a healthful diet. The problems arise when we eat too much food or too large a portion of a certain type of food or fat. For example, selecting a 3-ounce serving of lean beef is a good choice. Trimming the fat from meat is a good choice. Eating a 16-ounce serving of prime rib, including the fat, is a bad choice. Adding a couple of slices of avocado to a salad is a good choice; eating a whole avocado at one meal is a bad choice. A teaspoon of olive oil on a salad or a slice of bread is a good choice; half a cup of olive oil on that same salad or slice of bread is a bad choice.

The experts recommend that we limit our saturated fat to no more than 10 percent of our total calories. In order to do this we must limit the quantity of meat, whole-milk dairy products, and some tropical vegetable oils. This is one reason why the recommended portion size for a serving of meat is 3 ounces ready to eat and why nonfat or 1 percent milk is a better choice than whole milk or cream. Butter, coconut oil, lard, and ice cream all contain significant amounts of saturated fat.

Two other types of fat, monounsaturated and polyunsaturated fats, are generally considered "good" fats because they help lower cholesterol. They are found mostly in plant products and seafood. Avocado, olives, olive oil, and canola oil are all good sources of monounsaturated fat. Corn oil and safflower oil contain large amounts of polyunsaturated fat. All of these fats, regardless of their source, contain 9 calories per gram.

All Fats Are Not Created Equal

The fat we eat affects our cholesterol level. That is why the way food is prepared is so important. Boiled shrimp is high in cholesterol and low in fat, but when it is fried it is high in *both* cholesterol and fat. Generally, too much saturated fat in our diets tends to raise the cholesterol level in our blood. Polyunsaturated fat tends to lower our blood cholesterol. It lowers total cholesterol as well as HDL and LDL cholesterol. Monounsaturated in the diet has a beneficial effect on total cholesterol by lowering LDL cholesterol but does not lower HDL cholesterol. HDL is considered "good" cholesterol, so we do not want to lower it.

Olive oil is an example of a monounsaturated fat. It tends to have a positive effect on blood cholesterol, so it is usually considered a "good" fat. Nevertheless, it is important to remember that monounsaturated fat, yes even olive oil, contains calories, 9 in each gram. It doesn't take much to add up to a lot of calories, and extra calories translate to unwanted weight.

Trans-Fatty Acids

In the commercial food production process trans-fatty acids are produced when hydrogen is added to an unsaturated vegetable fat. After the fat has all the hydrogen it can hold, is it still considered a vegetable fat (which may have a beneficial effect on serum cholesterol), or is it a saturated fat (which may tend to raise serum cholesterol)? Some research indicates that trans-fatty acids may have the same effect on serum cholesterol as saturated fatty acids. How concerned should we be about the current controversy over the possible health hazards of dietary trans-fatty acids? The best advice that can be given at this time is to include trans-fatty acids as a part of your saturated fat allowance.

Food manufacturers have listened to the same information as you and I regarding trans-fatty acids. As a result, they have reformulated products traditionally high in trans-fatty acids to lower the amount of this fat. Tub or soft margarine is lower in trans-fatty acids than stick or hard margarine, and both types have less trans-fatty acids than they did twenty years ago. But some manufacturers are offering trans-free margarine both in stick and tub versions, so now you do have a choice. If you want to choose margarine, you can get it without the addition of trans-fatty acids.

Americans have increased the amount of vegetable fat and reduced the amount of animal fat they eat over the past few decades. Nonetheless, the amount of trans-fatty acids in the diet has remained relatively constant. This is because the primary sources of trans-fatty acids in the American diet are fried foods, stick or hard margarine, commercial baked goods, and commercial savory snacks such as snack chips and crackers. Trans-fatty acids are used in these foods because they do not spoil easily and thus help these foods last longer. Consumption of these foods has increased over the years. If you are concerned about eating trans-fatty acids you can cut way down on the amount you eat simply by eating fewer fried foods, snack foods, and commercial baked goods.

What Is Cholesterol?

Cholesterol is a fatlike substance that occurs naturally in all animals. Technically, it is classified as a lipid, a compound that is not soluble in water. Cholesterol and fat are both lipids, related but not quite the same. We all know that beef and pork and eggs contain cholesterol. So do fish, turkey, and chicken. Dietary cholesterol is found in all animal food products. Cholesterol is produced by the liver of all animals, including humans. Cholesterol is essential for the human body to function properly and make steroid hormones and bile acids. It helps build cell membranes and brain and nerve tissues. Our bodies produce all the cholesterol we need, so people who do not eat any animal products do not have to worry. However, some people manufacture more than they need. These are the folks who may need to take medication and watch their diet to control their cholesterol. The experts tell us that none of us should eat more than 300 milligrams of cholesterol a day. We will talk about what that means in terms of food a little later on in this chapter.

The amount and type of fat you eat and the way your body metabolizes that fat is very important. This is because people with diabetes are at greater risk for developing heart disease than people who do not have this disease. The experts haven't discovered the reason why this is true, but they do know it is true. This is why it is important that everyone with diabetes be concerned about the type and amount of fat they eat. It is also very important that you have a blood test at least once a year that measures total cholesterol levels as well as high-density lipoproteins (HDL), low-density lipoproteins (LDL), and triglycerides.

The primary food sources of cholesterol are organ meats, such as liver or kidney, egg yolk, and some shellfish. This is why people with elevated cholesterol are told to limit egg yolks to four a week and avoid organ meats. Both shrimp and lobster are relatively high in cholesterol but very low in fat. The way they are prepared makes a big difference. If you do eat lobster and shrimp, remember that boiled shrimp in a shrimp cocktail is a far better choice than fried shrimp. Try lobster in a salad or eaten with lemon, rather than dipped in butter.

Physical activity and/or exercise can influence your cholesterol level and may exert a greater influence on your serum cholesterol than the amount of dietary cholesterol you eat. That means that all of us have some control over our own cholesterol levels. We all have a different genetic makeup. Some people are more likely to have high cholesterol than others because of heredity. Some people need to take medication to control their cholesterol because they can't do it with diet and exercise alone. Making good food choices and exercising will help you improve your blood glucose, cholesterol levels, and overall health. Exercise can influence your HDL/LDL ratio, and besides it burns calories and will help you attain and maintain a reasonable body weight. The important issue is to keep your cholesterol under control.

What about Triglycerides?

Triglycerides are fat, whether they are in a salad dressing, in a frying pan, on your hips, or in your blood. One of the things we know about serum triglycerides is that they are strongly related to both glucose control and to obesity. Alcohol consumption raises serum triglycerides. Too much carbohydrate will also raise them. If you eat too many calories, whether they come from protein, fat, or carbohydrate, your triglycerides will go up.

This may seem like the bad news, but is it? If you think about it, triglycerides react a lot like blood glucose. So the same things you do to keep your blood glucose in good control will help keep your triglycerides under control as well. If you lose 5 pounds, you can help to lower both triglycerides and blood glucose!

Omega-3 Fatty Acids

Omega-3 fatty acids are polyunsaturated acids found primarily in fish. We learned about them when researchers were studying the Eskimo population. Even though they ate diets that were high in fat the Eskimos were not having heart attacks. They did eat lots of fish. Cold-water fish have higher levels of fat than tropical fish and they also have higher levels of omega-3 fatty acids. The research showed that omega-3 fatty acids were what helps prevent blood clots that may lead to heart attacks or stroke and may also help to prevent hardening of the arteries.

Since that discovery experts have recommended that we increase the amount of omega-3 fatty acids in our diet. One result of that recommendation was omega-3 supplements. These capsules have not proved as beneficial as their manufacturers had hoped they would. There is some evidence that shows fish oil supplements can interfere with glucose control. Therefore they are not recommended for people who have diabetes.

The good news is that the current research shows that we can benefit if we eat as few as 7 ounces of fish each week. The fish that have the highest amounts of omega-3 fatty acids are albacore tuna, salmon, mackerel, sardines, and lake trout. Canned fish is as good as fresh, but select fish that is packed in water, mustard, or tomato sauce for fewer calories. For most of us that translates into eating two or three fish meals in a week. Think about how you could prepare it without adding fat, such as poaching or baking.

Fat Replacers: Are They the Answer?

In the current low-fat era we can go to the grocery store and buy a wide variety of reduced-fat, low-fat, and fat-free products we had only dreamed of twenty years ago. The market is ripe for these products because it seems as if the whole world is trying to lose weight. Fat gram counting, like weight loss, may soon replace baseball as the national pastime.

Fat has important functions as an ingredient in food. For years we selected meat that was well marbled, because the fat makes the meat tender and contributes to its flavor. Fat is used as a lubricant in food preparation. It keeps food from sticking to the pan. This is why we "grease" a baking pan or put fat in the pan to fry an egg. It is the ingredient that is responsible for flaky piecrusts, light textured cakes, crisp french fries, and creamy ice cream. It also adds flavor and helps us feel full. Can we replace fat in some of the foods we eat? If you are observant in the grocery store, you will see that food manufacturers are making a valiant effort to do just that!

Any substance that replaces some of the fat in a food product can be termed a "fat replacer." Sometimes fat is replaced with water, for example, in a salad dressing. More frequently, fat is replaced with products that are carbohydrate-, protein-, or fat-based. These products are not necessarily calorie free. New fat replacers are appearing on the supermarket shelves on a regular basis.

Salatrim and caprenin are fat-based, reduced-calorie products. They provide 5 calories per gram. Olestra, also fat-based, is calorie free, because it is not absorbed by the body. Olestra's brand name is Olean, and it is approved for use in "savory snacks" like chips and crackers. Food products that contain it carry a warning label stating: "This product contains Olestra. Olestra may cause abdominal cramping and loose stools. Olestra inhibits the absorption of some vitamins and other nutrients. Vitamins A, D, E, and K have been added." Emulsifiers such as monoglycerides and diglycerides are also fat-based. They are not reduced in calories, but because they are used with water, less is needed, resulting in a lower fat product. You may find them in low-calorie salad dressings.

Protein-based fat replacers provide us with 4 calories per gram. They are made from egg white, milk, whey, soy, and other proteins. They cannot be used for frying and are usually found in frozen desserts because they provide a creamy texture.

Guar, gums, cellulose, and polydextrose are some of the carbohydrate-based fat replacers. The calories in these vary but can be as much as 4 calories per gram compared to the 9 calories per gam in fat. They thicken foods, and some mix with water to form a gel for a smooth texture. They are frequently used to replace fat in salad dressings and can be found in baked goods and other foods. Fruit purees and applesauce are also carbohydrates that can be used to replace fat in baked goods.

One thing we know for sure about fat replacers is that they are here to stay. The function a fat plays in a food will help you determine if and how a fat can be reduced or replaced. You can use a thickening agent like cornstarch in a sauce or gravy instead of using meat drippings or butter. You can use less fat in some items, using 1 percent or 2 percent milk instead of whole milk when making cream soup. You can use applesauce in place of oil when baking muffins. You may find a reduced-fat frozen dessert that satisfies you and has half the calories of ice cream. The important thing to remember is that if you eat a lot of low- and reduced-fat foods in place of grains, fruits, and vegetables you will end up with too many calories and too few nutrients. If carbohydrate is the fat replacer it may impact your blood glucose.

I have included a recipe for bran muffins to illustrate how you can reduce the amount of fat and change the type of fat you use in cooking and baking. When you alter recipes you must keep taste in mind. It usually works better to cut down on the amount of fat, particularly in a baked item, than to eliminate it altogether.

_____ Original Bran Muffins _____

Yield: 12 muffins

INGREDIENTS

1 cup sifted flour	1 egg
¼ cup sugar	⅔ cup whole milk
½ tsp. salt	¼ cup lard, melted
2½ tsps. baking powder	1½ cups All-Bran

Preheat oven to 400° F.

Spray muffin tin with baking spray or line a muffin tin with paper cups. Sift flour, sugar, salt, and baking powder into a bowl. In a separate bowl beat egg, add milk, lard (or oil and/or applesauce) and All-Bran. Add the sifted dry ingredients. Stir quickly, just until mixed. Do not beat. Mixture will be lumpy.

Fill muffin cups two-thirds full. Bake 25 to 30 minutes or until toothpick inserted into the center of a muffin comes out clean. Remove muffins from tin immediately. Cool on a rack.

NUTRITION FACTS

Serving size: 1 muffin
Starch exchanges: 1
Fat exchanges: 1
Calories: 124   Calories from
  fat: 49
Total fat: 5 grams
Saturated fat: 2 grams

Cholesterol: 24 milligrams
Sodium: 263 milligrams
Carbohydrate: 18 grams
Dietary fiber: 3 grams
Sugars: 6 grams
Protein: 3 grams

The original recipe contains 124 calories and 5 grams of fat for each muffin. The original recipe uses whole egg and melted lard. Below are the ingredients for three other versions of bran muffins with varying amounts of fat. The above directions apply to all versions.

Modified Bran Muffins

Yield: 12 Muffins

INGREDIENTS

1 cup sifted flour
¼ cup sugar
½ teaspoon salt
2½ teaspoons baking powder
1 egg

⅔ cup 2% milk
⅛ cup applesauce
1 ounce olive oil
1½ cups All-Bran

Directions: See above recipe for Original Bran Muffins.

NUTRITION FACTS

Serving Size: 1 muffin
Starch exchanges: 1
Calories: 95   Calories from fat: 19

Sodium: 263 milligrams
Carbohydrate: 18 grams
Dietary fiber: 3 grams

Total fat: 2 grams	Sugars: 6 grams
Saturated fat: 0 grams	Protein: 3 grams
Cholesterol: 19 milligrams	

The modified recipe contains 95 calories and 2 grams of fat for each muffin. This version uses a whole egg and replaces the lard with olive oil and applesauce. This modification replaces some of the saturated fat with monounsaturated fat as well as reduces the total fat in this recipe.

_____ Fat-Reduced Bran Muffins _____

Yield: 12 muffins

INGREDIENTS

1 cup sifted flour	1 egg
¼ cup sugar	⅔ cup 2% milk
½ tsp. salt	¼ cup applesauce
2½ tsps. baking powder	1½ cups All-Bran

Directions: See above recipe for Original Bran Muffins.

NUTRITION FACTS

Serving size: 1 muffin	Sodium: 263 milligrams
Starch exchanges: 1	Carbohydrate: 18 grams
Calories: 86 Calories from fat: 9	Dietary fiber: 3 grams
Total fat: 1 gram	Sugars: 6 grams
Saturated fat: 0 grams	Protein: 3 grams
Cholesterol 19 milligrams	

The fat-reduced recipe contains 86 calories and 1 gram of fat for each muffin. This version replaces all of the lard with applesauce, thereby lowering total fat and calories.

Fat-Free Bran Muffins

Yield: 12 muffins

INGREDIENTS

1 cup sifted flour
¼ cup sugar
½ tsp. salt
2½ tsps. baking powder

2 egg whites
⅔ cup skim milk
¼ cup applesauce
1½ cups All-Bran

Directions: See above recipe for Original Bran Muffins.

NUTRITION FACTS

Serving size: 1 muffin
Starch exchanges: 1
Calories: 80   Calories from fat: 0
Total fat: 0.36 grams
Saturated fat: 0 grams
Cholesterol: 0 milligrams

Sodium: 263 milligrams
Carbohydrate: 18 grams
Dietary fiber: 3 grams
Sugars: 6 grams
Protein: 3 grams

The fat-free recipe contains 80 calories and about ⅓ of a gram of fat for each muffin. This version uses egg whites instead of whole egg, applesauce instead of lard, and skim milk in place of 2 percent milk.

These examples show you how you can take a recipe and modify it to reduce the amount of fat it contains. It is very important to consider the quality and taste of the food when making changes in a recipe. You may find that the modified muffin does not taste any different from the original. However, if you switch to reduced fat or fat free the finished muffin may not be to your taste. The important thing is to pick reasonable changes you can live with. It may be a better choice to eat the modified muffin and feel satisfied than to select the fat free and feel deprived. Remember, it is up to you. If you want to eat a high-fat food, figure out how to fit that food into your overall diet. There are no good or bad foods, but there can be too much of a good thing!

Defining Fats and Fat Replacers

Fat and its relationship to good health can be confusing. The definitions provided here can help you sort out the facts.

Cholesterol: a waxy, fatlike substance essential to life.

Lipid: a chemical compound that is not soluble, that is, it will not dissolve in water.

Lipoprotein: a chemical compound made of a combination of both fat and protein that carries cholesterol in the blood.

HDL cholesterol: a lipoprotein that contains more protein than fat.

LDL cholesterol: a lipoprotein that contains more fat than protein.

VLDL cholesterol: a lipoprotein that carries triglycerides (fat) in the blood.

Dietary Cholesterol: cholesterol contained in the animal products in the diet. Dietary cholesterol does not directly correlate to serum or blood cholesterol.

Fat: a chemical compound that contains one or more fatty acids. It is also the primary form of energy (calorie) storage in the body.

Fatty acids: molecules made up of mostly hydrogen and carbon. They are also an essential component of fat.

Hydrogenated fat: a fat that has had hydrogen added to it to change its physical properties, usually to make it semisolid or heat stable. Margarine is an example of a hydrogenated fat.

Saturated fat: a fat that contains all the hydrogen atoms it can hold. Animal products are the main sources of saturated fat in the diet. Saturated fats in the diet tend to raise cholesterol in the blood.

Polyunsaturated fat: a fat that is missing one or more pairs of hydrogen atoms (contains one or more double bonds or places to attach hydrogen). Fats are also classified according to the position of the double bond; polyunsaturated fats have a double bond at the omega-6 position. Corn, sunflower, safflower, and soybean oils are the main sources of polyunsaturated fat in the diet.

Monounsaturated fat: a fat that is missing one pair of hydrogen atoms (contains one double bond or place to attach hydrogen). Fats are also classified according to the position of the double bond; monounsaturated fats have a double bond at the omega-9 position. Olive, canola, and peanut oils are the main sources of monounsaturated fat in the diet.

Omega-3 fatty acid: an unsaturated fat that is missing one pair of hydrogen atoms (contains one double bond or place to attach hydrogen). The missing double bond is at the omega-3 position, thus its name. Cold-water fish such as salmon, sardines, and mackerel are the main sources of omega-3 fatty acids in the diet.

Trans-fatty acid: a term referring to the position of the hydrogen atoms in relation to the double bond in a fat. "Cis" is a term that describes the typical placement of hydrogen atoms in a fatty acid, located on the same side of the carbon-to-carbon double bond. When a fat is hydrogenated, some of the hydrogen atoms move to the opposite (trans) side of the double bond. Trans-fatty acids are considered to be saturated fat in the diet. Hard margarine, fried snack foods and commercial baked products are the main sources of trans-fatty acids in the diet.

Fat Replacers

Noncaloric

Olean: a fatlike material with physical properties similar to fat. Made from esters of sucrose and long-chain fatty acids. The molecule is too large to be broken down in the normal digestive process. It passes through the digestive system intact and adds no energy (calories) to the diet. Can be used for frying.

Z-trim: an ingredient made from insoluble fiber in oats, soybeans, rice, or other grains. Z stands for zero calories. Cannot be used for frying.

Caloric (Fat-Based)

Salatrim: a combination of short- and long-chain fatty acids that is only partially absorbed by the body. It provides 5 calories per gram.

Caprenin: similar to salatrim, a combination of short- and long-chain fatty acids that is only partially absorbed by the body. Provides 5 calories per gram.

Emulsifiers: monoglycerides and diglycerides that create a suspension of one liquid in another. They allow manufacturers to blend ingredients that usually do not mix well such as water and oil. They provide 9 calories per gram but can be used in minute amounts to achieve a desired texture, so they add very few calories to the finished product and are used as an ingredient in "fat-free" foods.

Caloric (Protein-Based)

Simplesse, Trailblazer, Lita: microparticulated or microscopic-size particles of milk, egg, or whey protein that provide the creamy mouth feel of fat. Provide 1 to 5 calories per gram.

Caloric (Carbohydrate-Based)

Guar, Gums, Cellulose, Polydextrose, Maltodextrin, Modified food starch: examples of products that thicken, provide bulk, and/or a smooth texture. Provide up to 4 calories per gram. These were the first and most common fat substitutes.

Oatrim: made from oat flour and can be used in milk and processed meat as well as baked goods. Provides 4 calories per gram.

Understanding food labels, the topic of chapter 8, can help you use all you have learned about calories, sugar, carbohydrate, and fat to make healthful food choices.

Read Labels

Food labels provide a wealth of information for anyone who wants to know what is in the food they eat, but for people with diabetes, they are invaluable because they provide accurate information about the nutrients in food. Ever since May of 1994, consumers in this country have been able to go into a grocery store and find consistent information on all products bearing food labels. The label can tell you everything you need to know in order to make wise food choices. They are regulated by the Food and Drug Administration (FDA) and the Food Safety and Inspection Service (FSIS) of the U.S. Department of Agriculture (USDA) and must conform to strict standards. The FDA regulates almost all processed foods, except processed meat and poultry products, which are regulated by FSIS. These two agencies follow the same food-labeling regulations. All labels *must* provide ingredient labeling and a Nutrition Facts panel, and they *may* provide nutrient content claims and health claims.

Ingredient Labeling

If you have food allergies or any type of food intolerance, the most important thing to look at on the food label is the list of ingredients. This section of the label tells you exactly what is in the food and is crucial for anyone who has a severe reaction to a particular ingredient or wishes to avoid some substance for any reason. Ingredients are always listed starting with the most prevalent to the least.

Ingredient labeling provides a wealth of information to the person with diabetes, particularly to people who are looking for sugar on the list. If sugar in any form, such as sucrose (table sugar), corn syrup, dextrose, or honey, has been added to a food, it will be listed in the ingredient list. If more than one type of sugar has been added they will be grouped together. If sugar is naturally occurring it will not appear in the ingredient list but will be reflected in both the total carbohydrate and sugars listings on the Nutrition Facts panel.

Both naturally occurring and added sugar will affect your blood glucose, as both are carbohydrate. The kind of carbohydrate you eat is not as important as the total amount of carbohydrate. This is why you can incorporate table sugar into your diet if you include it as a part of the total carbohydrate you eat in a day. Let your blood glucose control be your guide as to how much carbohydrate you can eat.

Nutrition Facts

The Nutrition Facts label lists the serving size, the number of servings in the container, the amount of protein, total fat—including saturated fat—and cholesterol, carbohydrate—including fiber and sugars—sodium, vitamins A and

Nutrition Facts

A → Serving Size 1 cup (228g)
Servings Per Container 2

B → **Amount Per Serving**

Calories 260   Calories from Fat 120

	% Daily Value*
Total Fat 13g	
Saturated Fat 5g	**25%**
Cholesterol 30 mg	**10%**
Sodium 600 mg	**28%**
C → **Total Carbohydrate** 31g	**10%**
Dietary Fiber 0g	**0%**
Sugars 5g	
Protein 5g	**10%**

D →
Vitamin A	4%	•	Vitamin C	2%
Calcium	15%	•	Iron	4%

*Percent Daily Values are based on a 2,000 calorie
diet. Your daily values may be higher or lower
depending on your calorie needs:

	Calories:	2,000	2,500

E →
Total Fat	Less than	65g	80g
Sat Fat	Less than	20g	25g
Cholesterol	Less than	300mg	300mg
Sodium	Less than	2,400mg	
Total Carbohydrate	300g	375g	
Dietary Fiber		25g	30g

C, calcium, and iron. It also lists total calories, calories from fat, Percent Daily Values, and recommended total daily amounts for all nutrients listed. It designates the section of the label that contains specific, mandated nutrition information.

The A section of this panel contains the serving size and number of servings in each container. The serving size will be the same for the same type of product. For instance, all juice manufacturers must use one cup as the standard serving size. All the rest of the information on this panel relates to the serving size. If your serving size is different from the listed size, you need to get your calculator to figure out exactly what you are eating. For example, for most people with diabetes a serving of juice is $\frac{1}{2}$ cup, not 1 cup; therefore, all the other information needs to be cut in half to figure out what is in $\frac{1}{2}$ cup of juice.

Section B lists the number of calories in a serving of this item as well as the number of calories that come from fat in one serving. This information lets you figure out what percentage of the calories in this food come from fat. Merely divide the total calories per serving into the fat calories per serving and multiply that times 100 to get the percent of fat calories in this food. This is different from the percent of Daily Value of fat.

Section C tells the number of grams or milligrams of fat, saturated fat, cholesterol, sodium, total carbohydrate, fiber, sugars, and protein that are contained in one serving of this food. This is very helpful if you are trying to limit the amount of carbohydrate (or any of the listed nutrients) you eat or the amount you eat at a meal. The indented nutrients are components of those listed above them—saturated fat is part of the total fat, and dietary fiber and sugars are part of the total carbohydrate found in the food. The

FDA is working to add trans fat to this section. If they receive approval, any food that lists saturated fat will have to include trans fat in that total. The exact amount of trans fat will be designated by a footnote.

The amounts of specific vitamins and minerals are listed in section D as percentages of Daily Value. The panel must give this information for vitamins A and C, calcium, and iron. If the manufacturer makes a claim about any other nutrient or adds nutrients, then the percentage of Daily Values for those nutrients must be listed as well. Other nutrients that may be listed are vitamins D, E, B_6, B_{12}, thiamin, riboflavin, niacin, folate, biotin, pantothenic acid, phosphorus, iodine, magnesium, zinc, copper, and potassium.

The percent of Daily Value in section C tells you what percent of each nutrient of the total recommended for the entire day that one serving of this food provides. This percent is based on a reference 2,000-calorie diet. If your caloric goal is 1,500 calories each day these numbers are too high for you. You would need to aim for three-quarters of this amount. Do not fret over percent of Daily Value. It is easier to just look at total calories and the amount of major nutrients—like carbohydrate, fat, and cholesterol—that you are most concerned about.

Section E lists the recommended total daily amounts and is always the same when it appears on this panel. It refers to the recommended amount of the nutrients listed and is based on a 2,000- or 2,500-calorie diet. These numbers may be misleading to you, as most people with type 2 diabetes are concerned with losing weight and may be limiting their calories to 1,200 or 1,500 a day. The table on page 128 will show you how these numbers vary according to total calories.

Daily Values for Different Calorie Levels*

Calories		1,200	1,500	1,800	2,000	2,500
Total Fat	less than	40 grams	50 grams	60 grams	65 grams	80 grams
Sat. fat	less than	13 grams	16 grams	20 grams	20 grams	25 grams
Cholesterol	less than	300 mg	300 mg	300 mg	300 mg	300 mg
Sodium	less than	2,400 mg	2,400 mg	2,400 mg	2,400 mg	2,400 mg
Total Carbohydrate		180 grams	225 grams	270 grams	300 grams	375 grams
Dietary Fiber		20 grams	20 grams	21 grams	25 grams	30 grams

* Some numbers are rounded.

Recommendations for cholesterol and sodium are similar for all caloric levels. Note that they are maximum amounts and are worded as "less than." The National Cancer Institute is the group that makes the official recommendations for fiber, and it states that 20 grams is the minimum amount recommended.

One of the purposes of the 1994 law was to simplify the label. I know a lot of people who question whether or not the government agencies met that goal, but they did make food labeling uniform. That, in itself, is a real boon to people with diabetes. Once you have mastered all the intricacies of label reading you can use your knowledge on all labels. Food manufacturers do not have any discretion to be creative. Serving sizes cannot vary from manufacturer to manufacturer, and the Nutrition Facts panel makes it easy to compare nutrient information on similar products.

If you are interested in carbohydrates and sugars you can compare the information listed in section C of Nutrition Facts to the ingredient listing. There are a lot of foods that will not list sugar as an *ingredient* but that do list sugar as a *nutrient*. This is because the sugar is naturally occurring in these foods. Milk is a perfect example. The number of grams of sugars listed accounts for all of the carbohydrate in the milk. The same is true of fruit canned in juice, as all the carbohydrate comes from the sugar found in the fruit and juice. Remember, total carbohydrate is what you need to take into consideration when planning your meals. If a food has added sugar, it will be listed as an ingredient and appear as sugars under total carbohydrate. All sugar and all carbohydrate will raise your blood glucose whether it is naturally occurring or added as granulated sugar to the food, so you need to be more concerned with the total amount of carbohydrate you eat, rather than worrying about the source of the carbohydrate.

One of the most useful things about the Nutrition Facts panel is that it allows you to compare the nutrient composition of similar foods because the format in which the information is presented is consistent from product to product. You can hold containers of apple juice and orange juice side by side and decide which one of these will best meet your nutrient needs. With these facts you are now equipped to compare nutrition labels to help you select what you want and need.

Serving Size

Serving sizes are one of the most problematic things to deal with when you are concerned about getting the right amount of each nutrient. The FDA determined the serving sizes of foods by looking at the typical amount people eat, based on consumer surveys that are conducted by the government. As we all know in this "land of plenty" many Americans eat larger servings than they need. Consequently, the FDA and the American Diabetes Association and American Dietetic Association's *Exchange Lists for Meal Planning* do not always agree on how much constitutes a serving. If you are following a diabetes or weight loss meal plan, some label servings are too big for you. Juice illustrates my point. On the *Exchange Lists* ½ cup of apple, orange, grapefruit, pineapple, tomato, or vegetable juice is a serving. If you select cranberry, grape, or prune juice, ⅓ cup is a serving, whereas if you look at the Nutrition Facts panel on the food label a whole cup is a serving. This is very important for you to understand, as fruit juice can have a sizable effect on your blood glucose. If you decide to drink juice, the carbohydrate content of the juice determines your portion size. The amount of juice that provides 15 grams of carbohydrate is a serving. If you buy papaya nectar, which contains about 6 grams of carbohydrate in an ounce, 2½ ounces will provide 15 grams of carbohydrate. Apricot nectar contains roughly 5 grams of carbohydrate per ounce, and 3 ounces is a 15-gram carbohydrate serving, while carrot juice has only 2½ grams of carbohydrate per ounce, so 6 ounces give you your 15-gram carbohydrate serving.

Because the Nutrition Facts panel does list the serving in common household measures as well as metric, you can figure out how many calories are in 1 ounce and divide that number by 4 to determine the grams of carbohydrate in 1 ounce. When you buy a large container of juice, 16 ounces or more, the serving size will always be 1 cup or 8 ounces. If you purchase a 9-ounce container of juice the serving size will list the entire 9 ounces as one serving because the entire container is considered one serving. It is true that most people do not share the single serving container; however, if you have diabetes you need to consider how much carbohydrate you are getting out of the juice you are drinking. If your label stated that the 9-ounce container had 180 calories and 45 grams of carbohydrate you would know that it contained 3 servings for you.

The same is true of other foods you may eat. The *Exchange Lists* say that one serving of bread or starchy food contains 15 grams of carbohydrate and weighs 28 grams or 1 ounce. The FDA has deemed that 50 grams, almost 2 ounces, is a serving. This can get tricky when you are shopping, as bread and rolls come in so many different sizes. While 50 grams total weight is the official serving size, if a roll or slice of bread weighs 35 grams it will still be listed as 1 serving. The practical thing to do is look at the carbohydrate content of the item and count 15 grams as your serving size. It is important to distinguish between the number of grams of carbohydrate and the total gram weight of the product, as the total weight includes water and other things besides carbohydrate.

You will discover that the same thing is true of pasta and rice. The FDA serving size may not correspond to what your meal plan says you should eat. The label does give you all the information you need to figure out how much of the product it takes to give you your 15-gram carbohydrate serving.

If you want to eat snacks like potato chips or pretzels Nutrition Facts will help you figure out how much to eat. If you select chips, you need to figure the fat as well as the carbohydrate that this snack provides if you are concerned about your weight.

Snacks are marketed in either single or multi-serving packages, and the FDA serving size will vary according to the package size. The reason for this is a single-serving size package may vary from $\frac{1}{2}$ ounce to as much as 2 ounces of the same snack, and the average person eats the entire single serving package. If the snack chips are in a multi-serving package, the serving size is 1 ounce. The *Exchange List* serving size is the same, regardless of the packaging. Nutrition Facts gives you the information you need to make an informed decision about your food choices.

If you eat luncheon or packaged meats you will see that the FSIS has deemed that 2 ounces are a serving. If you follow the *Exchange Lists* the serving size is 1 ounce, and *The First Step in Diabetes Meal Planning* says 2 to 3 ounces is a serving. What are you supposed to do? I think the easiest way to handle meat or protein food is to look at the number of ounces you want to eat in a day. For most people, that is 6 ounces. If the Nutrition Facts panel says a serving is 2 slices and weighs 2 ounces then you know that each slice is 1 ounce and you can decide how many ounces you want to eat at that meal.

Fat is the other category where you will find a big difference between what the FDA and the *Exchange Lists* call one serving. If you recall, the FDA determined serving size based on what Americans are eating. They say a serving of fat is one tablespoon. That is three times as much as the one teaspoon–size serving you will find in the *Exchange Lists*. This is very important to keep in mind if you are watching calories as well as carbohydrate because fat has 9 calories per gram, and they add up in a hurry. Five grams of fat or 45 calories' worth of fat are what you should count as a serving. If you purchase salad dressing and the Nutrition Facts panel says that it contains 14 grams of fat per serving, you would count it as 3 servings (not 1 serving) of fat. All you have to do is divide the number of grams of fat listed on the label by five to determine how many servings of fat you will get if you eat the label-size serving.

Nutrient Content Claims

A nutrient claim on a food label is a word or phrase that describes the amount of a nutrient in the food. Nutrient claims have to meet strict definitions for these terms, which may also be referred to as descriptors. Examples of nutrient claims are terms like "lean," "low-fat," "high," "good source," "sugar-free," and "no cholesterol." These claims address both the nutrients we are likely to get more of than we need, like fat and cholesterol, as well as those nutrients that we want to ensure an ample supply of in our daily diet, like calcium and fiber. A food package cannot carry these terms unless the product meets very specific guidelines. The good thing about these claims is that no matter where they appear, the words always mean the same thing.

Nutrient content claims can be either absolute or comparative. "Free" is an absolute claim, whereas "reduced" is a comparative claim. Both of these terms, as well as any others that are used, have strict definitions. The chart below gives the definitions for the absolute claims of "free" and "low."

Nutrient Content Claim Definitions*

Free	Nutrient	Low
0.5 grams of fat or less	Fat	3 grams of fat or less
0.5 grams saturated fat or less	Saturated fat	1 gram saturated fat or less
less than 2 milligrams of cholesterol and 2 grams or less of saturated fat	Cholesterol	20 milligrams of cholesterol or less and 2 grams or less of saturated fat
less than 5 milligrams of sodium	Sodium	35 milligrams or less of sodium for very low sodium, and 140 milligrams of sodium or less for low sodium
less than 5 calories	Calories	40 calories or less
less than 0.5 grams	Sugar	may not be used as a nutrient content claim

*If a product has a very small serving size, less than 50 grams, these definitions apply to 50-gram amounts.

Sometimes other acceptable terms—like "no fat," "free of sodium," "zero sugar" "or "sugarless"—may be used to indicate "free" foods. If the term implies free, the product must meet the definition listed.

If a product claims that it is reduced or has less fat, saturated fat, sodium, calories, and/or sugar then it will have at least 25 percent less than the regular product. If the manufacturer wants to make this claim for cholesterol then the food must have at least 25 percent less cholesterol and no more than 2 grams of saturated fat. This is because saturated fat in a food can affect your cholesterol level.

In order to be called "lean," meat, poultry, and seafood must have less than 10 grams of fat, 4 grams of saturated fat, and 95 milligrams of cholesterol per serving and/or 100 grams. This is also true of main dish or entrée items. The same size portions must have fewer than 5 grams of fat, 2 grams of saturated fat, and 95 milligrams of cholesterol to qualify for the "extra lean" label.

"Light" or "lite" refer to more than color and when they mean calories these words designate a product that contains $\frac{1}{3}$ fewer calories or 50 percent less fat than the original version. If more than half the calories in the item come from fat, the fat content of the product must be reduced by 50 percent or more to be called "light" or "lite." If these words are used to describe either color or texture the label must specify "light" in color or "light" in texture.

Sometimes you see a product like luncheon meat labeled 97 percent fat-free or 95 percent lean. The percent-free or percent-lean label can be used if the product meets all the requirements for a low-fat food that are listed on the preceding table. If the product is labeled 100 percent fat-free it must meet all the requirements for fat-free listed previously, have less than $\frac{1}{2}$ gram of fat in 100 grams, and contain no added fat.

Low-sodium and low-calorie claims can be made for main dish or entrée items if the product has fewer than 140 milligrams of sodium or contains fewer than 120 calories in a 100-gram serving. One hundred grams is 3½ ounces.

Any product that contains between 10 percent and 19 percent of the Daily Value of a nutrient can claim to be a good source of that nutrient. The Daily Value for vitamin A is 5,000 IU. A "good source of vitamin A" claim could be made for a product that contains between 500 (10 percent) and 950 (19 percent) IU of Vitamin A in a serving.

In order to make the claim of "excellent source of," "high," or "rich in" the product must contain 20 percent or more of the Daily Value of the nutrient in each serving. Using our vitamin A example, the product would have to have 1,000 IU of vitamin A in each serving.

The most recently approved nutrient claim is for using the term "healthy." In order for a food to be labeled "healthy" it must be low in both fat and saturated fat, and contain no more than 480 milligrams of sodium and 60 milligrams of cholesterol per serving. This food must also provide at least 10 percent of the Daily Value for vitamins A or C, or iron, calcium, protein, or fiber.

Health Claims

For the first time ever, health claims, messages, or statements that describe a relationship between a food or a component of a food and the risk of a health-related condition or a disease are regulated by the government. When Congress passed the Nutrition Education and Labeling Act of 1990 it gave FDA and FSIS regulators the power to make health claims consistent.

A health claim is a powerful message, and food companies vie to be able to make these claims. But like everything else related to food labeling, they must meet strict guidelines. It may be a written statement, a description, or even take the form of a symbol such as a heart, a popular choice if the health claim refers to coronary heart disease or hypertension.

Currently, the diseases or health-related conditions for which health claims can be made are limited to cancer, coronary heart disease, hypertension, osteoporosis, neural tube defects, and dental caries. This list will grow as research documents evidence for additional claims. Health claims are authorized for diet and health relationships that are backed by sound scientific evidence. Manufacturers use health claims to market their products. The primary purpose is to benefit consumers by providing information on healthful eating patterns that may help reduce the risk of disease. FDA-approved health claims that producers, manufacturers, and marketers may use are limited to:

- Fruits and vegetables and reducing the risk of cancer.
- Fruits, vegetables, and grain products that contain fiber, particularly soluble fiber that may reduce the risk of coronary heart disease.
- Fiber-containing grain products, fruits, vegetables and reducing the risk of cancer.
- Dietary fat and reducing the risk of cancer.
- Dietary saturated fat and cholesterol and reducing the risk of coronary heart disease.
- Sodium and reducing the risk of hypertension or high blood pressure.
- Calcium and reducing the risk of osteoporosis.
- Folate and reducing the risk of neural tube defects.
- Dietary sugar alcohols and reducing the risk of dental caries (cavities).

- Dietary soluble fiber, such as that found in whole oats and psyllium seed husks, and reducing the risk of coronary heart disease.
- Diets rich in whole-grain foods and other plant foods that are low in total fat, saturated fat, and cholesterol may help reduce the risk of heart disease and certain cancers.
- Dietary soy protein and reducing the risk of heart disease.

Health Claim Requirements

Health claims show a relationship between a nutrient or other substance and a disease or health-related condition. In order to qualify for a health claim, a food must be high in healthful nutrients and low in those most of us try to limit like fat, saturated fat, cholesterol, and sodium. These regulations limit foods that can make such claims.

The regulators have come up with specific claims that can be used and the manufacturer must include all the components of the model health claim on the label. Cereal is a naturally low-fat food and may meet the qualifications and make a claim. I have included a direct quote from a cereal label to illustrate this point.

> While the development of heart disease depends on many factors, diets low in saturated fat and cholesterol *may reduce the risk of heart disease.* Original Nabisco Shredded Wheat and Grape-Nuts have *no saturated fat and no cholesterol.* See other side for nutrition information. These products meet the American Heart Association dietary guidelines for healthy people over age two when used as part of a balanced diet.

These cereals provide 21 percent Daily Value for fiber and are within the sodium limits, so they qualify for a health claim. The wording always includes a reference to reducing risk rather than being a cure-all.

There are no health claims that apply specifically to diabetes because there is no scientific evidence that ties a specific food or food component to the risk of developing diabetes. Nevertheless, if a food carries any health claim then that food is probably a good choice. Labels on food contain all the nutrient information you need to make informed food choices. The information on ingredients, nutrient breakdown, nutrient content claims and health claims is consistent from product to product and makes comparisons simple. Use this information to plan healthful meals and snacks to help control your blood glucose.

Everything you learn about food, ingredients, and food labels helps you to make healthful choices. In chapter 9, all this information is applied to modifying traditional recipes.

Don't Give Up Your Comfort Food

All of us have foods that evoke good memories. Grandma's special blueberry cobbler still warm from the oven brings back visions of carefree summer childhood days. In this chapter, you will learn how it is possible to figure out how you can still enjoy your favorite foods while maintaining good blood glucose control.

I hope that by this point you are considering including a favorite food as a challenge rather than a "cheat." I have not used that term up to this point because I do not think it should be used when we are discussing food or diabetes self-management. *Webster* defines *cheating* as "the act of deceiving or swindling; deception; fraud or to deal with dishonesty for one's own gain." I do not think eating too large a serving of any food fits in this category.

There are several things you can do to enjoy all your favorite foods. You can experiment to see how the food affects your blood glucose and make adjustments in portion or meal size. You can do a reality check to see if the food

Modify Mom's Pie

really is as great or as good as you remember, and if so, how can you fit it in. Or you can look at the recipe and make some modifications that change the effect of the food on your blood glucose. Another alternative may be to start some new traditions and create your own new comfort foods.

Check Your Glucose

Let's briefly review the steps you need to take to find out how a particular food affects your blood glucose.

● Check your blood glucose before you eat.
● Record that number.
● Eat the food in question.

- Check your blood glucose 30 minutes after you have finished eating the food.
- Record that number.
- Check your blood glucose 2 hours (1½ hours after the first check) after you have finished eating the food.

If your blood glucose is under 200 mg/dl at this point and has not gone higher than 200, you have learned that the food in question, in the portion size selected, is okay for you.

If your numbers are too high you need to stop and figure out what options are available to lower those numbers. One option might be to eat a smaller portion of that particular food. Another might be to eat smaller servings of other items in the meal to make room for the favorite food. Another strategy is to assess these foods and decide if they really are as good as the memories.

Check Your Memories

I will share my own experience of favorite foods as an example. I am from a large family and our home was always full of people, especially for holidays and other special occasions. My mother was a wonderful cook and excelled at baking. One of her specialties was homemade apple pie. When I was a child and she made pie, it was always eaten for dessert, and there were enough people at the dinner table that there was never any leftover pie. As a result of these childhood experiences, the only time I will eat pie is if it is fresh from the oven. If it was baked yesterday or has been in the refrigerator overnight, it cannot be as good as my mother used to make. As a result, if I am offered pie, I assess the situation, and if it does not meet my self-imposed criteria for being as good as mother used to make, I simply say no, thank you.

I have decided not to spend my calories on any pie that doesn't match my mother's. I may have missed some delicious pie in my life, but that is okay because I have never felt deprived.

I also have transferred my pie philosophy to other foods, especially high-calorie foods and try to ask myself, "Is this worth the calories?" Sometimes the answer is yes, a lot of the times the answer is no. The more you practice this, the more discriminating you will become, and pretty soon it will be second nature. You are in control when you decide what you want to eat, rather than eating just because the food is available.

How can you put this strategy into practice in your own life? For example, if you love chocolate, decide that only the best is good enough for you. Perhaps you occasionally decide to treat yourself to imported chocolate, because domestic chocolate just does not meet your criteria. Now you have put yourself in control. When you are tempted to buy that candy bar out of the machine at work, you can turn it down because it is not imported chocolate, rather than telling yourself you will "cheat" just this once! If this is going to work for you, you must be selective in your criteria and make them strict enough so that you will not be faced with your favorite foods on a daily basis. But your criteria should allow you the flexibility to have what you really want occasionally.

Analyze all the foods that Mother or Grandma used to make that you put into the "comfort food" category, that is, any food from your childhood that you remember fondly. Then check the recipe, as it is possible that some of these foods are just fine the way Mom made them and do not need any modifications. Other foods may be high in fat, cholesterol, sugar, and sodium and can be modified to lower the content of these nutrients while still meeting your taste criteria. Remember that your tastes may have changed over the years.

Modify Your Recipes

If yours is a family that has traditions of favorite pastries or cookies that are a part of a holiday celebration, don't despair. Instead, become a "kitchen chemist." Look at the recipes for these goodies and experiment with changes. It has been my experience that a lot of the old family recipes can be adapted so that many times no one even knows the difference. Some recipes do not lend themselves to change, so we will talk about what you can change and what is best left alone.

Every recipe is a chemical formula. It lists the ingredients in the product, the amount of each of the ingredients, and how to put these ingredients together to make a satisfactory item. Food companies and cookbook publishers spend a great deal of time and money standardizing recipes so that the finished product is the same every time. If you change a standardized recipe the product will be different from the one that was tested and published. Unless your grandmother wrote cookbooks, she did not standardize her recipes, and family favorites varied from year to year. Many of Grandma's recipes were passed down by oral tradition and called for a pinch of this or a handful of that and what was in season, and they were not all that precise to begin with, so feel free to experiment.

Recipes can be modified by **reducing** the quantity of some ingredients, by **substituting** one ingredient for another, or by **omitting** an ingredient altogether. For example, you could use ½ cup in place of ¾ cup of chopped nuts, substitute Equal for some of the sugar, and omit the salt entirely and still have a very satisfactory cookie. Let's look at specific ingredients.

Sugar

If you are concerned about sugar you might wonder how you can reduce the amount you use in baking. First of all, sugar has some specific qualities in baking that you should be familiar with. Every yeast dough recipe calls for sugar; it may be as little as a teaspoon, but this small amount is necessary for the yeast to work properly to make the dough rise. Sugar gives tenderness to these products as well as helps them develop the golden brown crust we all love. It does not take very much sugar to produce these qualities, but it does take some, so the rule here is to reduce the sugar but not omit it entirely. Sugar also contributes volume to cake, and if you reduce it too much, it will result in an unfamiliar texture. You can usually reduce the sugar in a baked item like cake by one-third without seeing much of a difference in the end results. If a recipe calls for 1 cup of sugar, you should be able to cut that to $\frac{2}{3}$ of a cup. If you are baking cake, try using no more than $\frac{1}{2}$ cup sugar per 1 cup of flour. Experiment, as you may get a very satisfactory product with as little as $\frac{1}{4}$ cup of sugar per cup of flour. If you are baking cookies you may be able to use $\frac{1}{4}$ cup sugar or even less per cup of flour. Flavorings like vanilla or almond and spices such as cinnamon and nutmeg can help to enhance flavor when sugar is reduced.

If texture and volume are not in question, it is easy to substitute a sugar replacer to get the desired sweet taste. A packet of a sugar replacer like Equal or Sweet'n Low are equivalent to two teaspoons of sugar, so it is important to use the proper quantity in any substitution.

I will demonstrate updating a recipe, using blueberry cobbler as an example.

_____ Grandma's Blueberry Cobbler _____

Yield: 6 servings

INGREDIENTS

16 ounces frozen blueberries	1 Tbsp. sugar
1 Tbsp. flour	6 Tbsp. butter
½ cup sugar	1 egg
1 cup flour	½ cup cream
2 tsps. baking powder	Butter to "grease" 6-by-10-
1 tsp. salt	inch baking dish

Preheat oven to 400°F.

Grease baking dish. Let blueberries thaw until they separate. Mix 1 tablespoon flour and ½ cup sugar into blueberries and put mixture into the prepared baking dish.

Sift together 1 cup flour, baking powder, salt, and 1 tablespoon sugar. Melt butter, let cool, and mix with egg and cream; add mixture to dry ingredients. Mix until dry ingredients are moistened. Mixture will be lumpy. Spoon dough onto berry mixture. Bake for fifteen minutes at 400°F, then reduce oven temperature to 350°F and bake ten more minutes or until the crust is golden brown. Remove from oven. Serve while still warm. If desired, top with sweet or whipped cream.

NUTRITION FACTS
(FIGURES DO NOT INCLUDE SWEET OR WHIPPED CREAM)

Serving size: ⅙ of recipe, about ⅔ of a cup	Cholesterol: 75 milligrams
Starch exchanges: 4	Sodium: 687 milligrams
Saturated fat exchanges: 3	Carbohydrate: 59 grams
Calories: 388 Calories from fat: 144	Dietary fiber: 3 grams
Total fat: 16 grams	Sugars: 38 grams
Saturated fat: 9 grams	Protein: 4 grams

_____ Modified Blueberry Cobbler _____

Yield: 6 servings

INGREDIENTS

1 16-ounce package frozen
  blueberries
1 Tbsp. flour
12 packets of Equal*

1 cup Bisquick
½ cup plus 1 Tbsp. 2% milk
3 Tbsp. vegetable oil
Cooking spray

Preheat oven to 400°F.

Spray 6-by-10-inch baking dish with cooking spray. Let blueberries thaw until they are separated. Mix flour and Equal into the blueberries and put mixture into prepared baking dish.

Add milk and oil to Bisquick; mix until dry ingredients are moistened. Mixture will be lumpy. Spoon dough onto berry mixture. Bake for fifteen minutes at 400°F, then reduce oven temperature to 350°F and bake ten more minutes or until the crust is golden brown. Remove from oven. While still warm, serve with milk or whipped topping.

*12 packets of Equal provide the sweetening value of 24 teaspoons of sugar. There are 3 teaspoons in a tablespoon, and 16 tablespoons in a cup, so 24 teaspoons of Equal provide the sweetening value of 8 tablespoons or ½ cup of sugar.

NUTRITION FACTS
(FIGURES DO NOT INCLUDE MILK OR WHIPPED TOPPING)

Serving size: ⅙ of recipe,
  about ⅔ cup
Starch exchanges: 1½
Fat exchanges: 2
Calories: 206   Calories
  from fat: 97
Total fat: 11 grams
Saturated fat: 2 grams

Cholesterol: 2 milligrams
Sodium: 260 milligrams
Carbohydrate: 24 grams
Dietary fiber: 3 grams
Sugars: 7 grams
Protein: 4 grams

The most significant modification that I made in this recipe was to replace the sugar with Equal. This change reduced the sugars in this dessert 16 grams per serving. I used Bisquick rather than flour, baking powder, and salt, and this substitution reduced the carbohydrate still further. Other changes include vegetable oil rather than butter, 2 percent milk in place of cream, and eliminating the egg. All of these changes reduced the total fat, saturated fat, cholesterol, and sodium.

This recipe makes 6 servings. If you live alone or there are only two of you, this may become a problem, as most people will eat all of the cobbler, even if they do so over two or three days. I realized this after I made the cobbler, tried it, and then put the rest in the refrigerator and my husband just couldn't resist the leftovers. He suggested I try to make a smaller batch. I did and it worked out great.

_____ Modified Blueberry Cobbler _____

Yield: 2 servings

INGREDIENTS

5 ounces frozen blueberries   3 Tbsp. 2% milk
¾ tsp. flour   1 Tbsp. vegetable oil
4 packets Equal   Cooking spray
⅓ cup Bisquick

Use two individual Pyrex custard cups for baking. Follow the directions for the 6-serving version of the Modified Blueberry Cobbler. The Nutrition Facts are the same.

I made some modifications to the fat in this recipe, although cutting down on the oil and using skim milk in place of 2 percent milk could further reduce it. What I really wanted you to see is how easy it is to use a calorie-free sugar substitute in a fruit-based dessert like a cobbler or a pie and have this substitution make a substantial difference in the sugars, carbohydrate, and calories without appreciably changing the taste.

All of the calorie-free sugar replacers currently available have some limitations in replacing table sugar in a recipe, with the major problem being the lack of bulk. I recommend you follow the lead of the manufacturers, as they rarely use a single source of sweetening in a product. For home use, particularly if you are baking, try combining a calorie-free sweetener with table sugar. If you are making a dessert sauce that you will thicken with flour, cornstarch, or tapioca, such as the cobbler above, you can generally use the calorie-free sweetener exclusively. If you decide to replace table sugar with granulated fructose you will end up with very little, if any, caloric difference.

Once you start experimenting with your favorite recipes you will discover that this process is not all that difficult. Make changes a little at a time. I guarantee your family will not detect many of the changes you make. The important thing you must remember is to write down what you do. If you get something "just perfect" with half the sugar you want to make sure you can repeat the results. Do not be disheartened if every effort isn't a smashing success, but don't give up, because practice really does make perfect and perseverance will pay off.

Fat

There are lots of ways you can modify recipes to reduce the amount of fat. Start off by looking at your recipe to see how you can reduce the fat, substitute another ingredient for the fat or some of the fat, and finally, omit the fat altogether. If you want to modify the amount of fat you use in a baked item you have to look at the role the fat plays in the final product. You can make a fat-free muffin or quick bread by substituting applesauce or mashed banana measure for measure in the recipe. For example, if the muffin recipe calls for $\frac{1}{2}$ cup vegetable oil, you can use $\frac{1}{2}$ cup applesauce instead. This works particularly well if the muffins or quick bread will be eaten soon after they are baked, as the fruit puree muffins will dry out more quickly than those made with vegetable oil. You also need to understand that if you substitute fruit puree for fat you are decreasing the fat you eat, but you are also increasing the amount of carbohydrate you will eat. You need to take the increased carbohydrate into account if you wish to keep your blood glucose under control.

There are times you may want to substitute oil for a solid shortening. If your recipe says to chill the fat or have it below a certain temperature, then it is not a good idea to use a liquid fat in place of a solid one. The chilled, solid fat contributes to the flakiness of the baked piecrust, puff pastry, or biscuits. If the recipe calls for melted shortening, you should measure the shortening after melting, and in these instances, you may be able to substitute. The thing to remember is that oil is 100 percent fat while margarine has some water in it, so if you substitute oil for margarine you will end up with a higher fat product.

If you wish to use a reduced-calorie or light margarine in a recipe, you must take into account that a light margarine contains more water than regular margarine, so the amount of other liquid in the recipe must be reduced as well. This substitution can be tricky when baking, so you might try to reduce the fat by just using less regular margarine, then you will not have to adjust the amount of liquid in the recipe and you will still save total calories.

If you are making gravy, you can skim the fat from the drippings before you make the gravy. Every tablespoon of fat that you discard contains approximately 120 calories. If your homemade soup is among your comfort foods you can cut fat and throw away lots of calories by skimming the fat. The easiest way to do this is to chill your meat or poultry stock before you add vegetables and starch to your soup. Once the stock is chilled, the fat comes off in big chunks. If you measure the fat you discard you know how many calories you threw away. And I ask you, can you think of anything more satisfying than "throwing calories away"? It sure beats eating them!

If you are making a creamed soup you can save lots of calories and fat by using evaporated skim milk rather than cream, whole milk, or 2 percent milk. Your soup will be just as "creamy" as if you had a higher fat dairy product. You can puree vegetable, potato, or rice to thicken soup if it is too thin.

Another thing you can do to throw away fat is to carefully trim all the fat from any meat or poultry prior to cooking or certainly prior to eating. Keep the 120 calories per tablespoon in mind and you will find this task much easier to do. I am reminded of the first time that my husband saw me skinning a chicken. He was horrified that I was throwing so much away. So we got the kitchen scales out and learned that the whole chicken with all its skin weighed 2 pounds, 8 ounces, and had about 1,500 calories. After removing all the skin and visible fat the poor naked chicken weighed 2 pounds and now had about 600 calories. The reason the weight didn't go down more was because we left the bones in the chicken. What we removed was the skin and all the fat we could take off, totaling about 900 calories. When he learned the facts, he was happy to discard all those calories.

The same thing is true of virtually any type of meat or poultry you prepare. Next time you buy a steak or pork chops look at the amount of fat the butcher leaves on and figure out how much of that you can trim off. All you need is a cutting board and a sharp knife. Every tablespoon of fat you trim saves about 120 calories from your waist and hips. Or if you want to weigh the fat you plan to discard you can count 250 calories per ounce. You can challenge yourself to see how many calories you can trim from your meals by literally cutting the fat.

You can also cut down by not adding fat when you prepare foods. If you use nonstick cookware, you can pan broil or "fry" a piece of meat without adding any fat to the pan. All meat has a certain amount of fat and this fat melts when the meat reaches a high enough temperature. So if you put your meat into a dry pan as the meat heats up enough fat cooks out to lubricate the pan and also helps brown the meat. Do not hesitate to try other low-fat preparation methods such as steaming, broiling, poaching, roasting, and baking. Use your backyard barbecue to grill foods without adding fat. If you use these cooking methods, you will not have to add additional fat in cooking. Marinate lean meat in low-fat or fat-free liquids to tenderize and add flavor to meat. Lemon juice, tomato juice, nonfat milk, and nonfat salad dressings are all examples of low-fat marinades.

Try leaner versions of your favorite recipes. If you like chili, it is easy to make your homemade version lower in fat than what you would purchase. A can of a popular brand of chili without beans contains two servings at 410 calories each. A whopping 270 of those calories come from fat. If you make chili from scratch the recipe may recommend that you brown your ground meat in fat. You know that you do not have to do that! You can start with very lean ground meat and brown it in a nonstick skillet and drain off any fat that cooks out of the meat. The easiest way to do this is to drain the ground meat in a large strainer and rinse it with boiling water. Now that you have removed as much fat as possible, add the rest of your ingredients; the tomatoes, kidney beans, and seasonings will add a minimal amount of fat to the finished product. The flavor of the ingredients and seasonings will predominate, rather than the taste of fat.

Check to see how much fat you add to food. You may do it many times from force of habit as much as from taste. Do you put butter or sauce on your vegetables? Think about other alternatives like seasoned salt or butter-flavored salt if you do not have to watch your sodium intake. A squeeze of lemon juice brings out the flavor without adding calories or sodium. A teaspoon of grated Parmesan cheese will add 8 calories, while an ounce of cheese sauce can add between 50 and 100 calories. A teaspoon of butter or margarine adds the same number of calories to your baked potato as two tablespoons of sour cream. Think about that, as one teaspoon of butter or margarine does not go very far on a baked potato. You could add ¼ cup of salsa to the potato. Salsa is considered a free food because it is so low in calories.

Salt

Many people who have diabetes may also have hypertension and as a result be concerned about the amount of salt and sodium they consume. The American Diabetes Association recommendation for sodium intake for people with diabetes is the same as for the general population, less than 3,000 milligrams a day. People with hypertension, whether they have diabetes or not, should consume less than 2,400 milligrams of sodium (about 1 teaspoon of table salt) a day.

So if you modify recipes to reduce sodium, you are helping the whole family.

Historically, salt was used to preserve foods before we had modern refrigeration or preservation methods. As a result, we have developed a taste for salt and most of us use too much. Think about that when you think about modifying recipes, as most of the salt is added "to taste" rather than because it is essential to the recipe. Salt is very definitely an acquired taste, so once you start to reduce the amount you eat, you will want less. That fact helps you when you change a recipe.

If you bake yeast bread or rolls *do not* eliminate salt entirely from these products, as it is an essential ingredient for both flavor and texture. The easiest way to reduce salt is to cut down on the amount the recipe calls for. That is, if a recipe calls for 1 teaspoon of salt you can use ¾ or ½ teaspoon instead. This will be more acceptable to your family if you gradually reduce the amount of salt each time you make the recipe. Also salt added at the very end of cooking will yield a "saltier" flavor than if you add it at the beginning. The same is true of salt added at the table. The problem there, of course, is how do you know how much you have used? Many times, salting at the table is done out of habit rather than taste. In our house we have plugged up all but one hole in every saltshaker, so that if we add salt, the amount is automatically limited.

Commercially prepared soup has traditionally been high in sodium. Unfortunately, as consumers we like it that way. Several years ago Campbell's made a big push with salt-free soups, and they were a market failure. When the sodium was all but eliminated the soup just didn't taste right so the product did not sell. When they came back on the market with Healthy Request soups consumers accepted them. The Healthy Request soups are 30 percent lower in sodium than the regular canned soup. When I compared labels in the store the can of Healthy Request had 480 milligrams of sodium per serving while the regular had between 900 and 980 milligrams per serving. The lesson here is twofold: if you are shopping read the label; if you are cooking and modifying a recipe, use moderation. Small, gradual changes are usually accepted and many times not even noticed by your family, while radical changes may bring rejection.

Once you start thinking about modifying recipes you will find all sorts of ways you can cut the amount of sugar, fat, and salt you eat without sacrificing flavor. You will soon become an expert at updating traditional family favorite recipes so that you can enjoy your comfort foods and at the same time cut the sugar, fat, and salt.

You have learned a lot about shopping, food preparation, and even how to modify recipes, but what do you do in a restaurant? Chapter 10 helps you learn what you need to know.

Eating Out Healthfully

One of the first concerns many people have after learning that they have diabetes is what they can eat in a restaurant. You may wonder whether you can still meet your nutritional needs when you eat in restaurants, which has become a way of life for many of us. Will you be able to control your blood glucose on the days when you eat out?

The most important thing to remember when you go to a restaurant is that you are paying for the food and so you should be able to get what you want. You are the customer and should select a restaurant that offers the type of foods you want and need. It is not realistic to expect a fast-food restaurant to prepare foods that are not listed on their menu or for an ethnic restaurant to offer foods of a different culture. However, these days the smart restaurant managers do their best to cater to their clientele in order to keep them coming back.

Think about the kind of food you like to eat and the restaurants you have been patronizing before you developed diabetes. Your tastes will not change because you have diabetes, but what you can change is your approach to satisfying your taste. It is up to you to become an informed consumer and find out how your favorite restaurant prepares your favorite dish and figure out how much of it will fit into your meal plan. I have a firm belief that a calorie is a terrible thing to waste, especially in a restaurant. Consequently, it is crucial that you do not waste them on just ordinary food. Become a food critic. If you taste something and it isn't wonderful, do not eat it. If you take a bite of something and push it away, most good restaurants will offer you something else, as they want you to be satisfied. If you take one bite and are dissatisfied, tell your server. If the server cannot take care of the problem, ask for the check. Ninety-nine times out of 100 the manager will instantly appear and resolve the problem. If that does not happen leave the food rather than jeopardize your blood glucose control. Your health is more important than the money you will lose. If a restaurant does not serve the food the way you like it, you know not to patronize them in the future.

Many restaurateurs realize that the more often people eat out the more they are concerned with fat, cholesterol, sugar, and calories at those meals. Some people are concerned about what they eat because they have a chronic condition such as heart disease, hypertension, or diabetes. Others just want to make healthy choices in restaurants because they know that what they eat contributes to their overall health and they do not want to develop high cholesterol or other health problems. Smart restaurant owners are ready and willing to cater to these groups, as they are all competing for this business.

How to Order

The first rule of survival in a full-service restaurant is: don't be afraid to ask!! Tell the server you have diabetes or you are watching your weight and ask for suggestions for lighter items. If you really want to know what those gourmet chefs put in the food you need to ask, ask, ask!! Be sure to keep in mind that the biggest obstacles to healthful choices are the size of the portion and the amount of fat that is added to the food during preparation.

Ask:

- How large is this portion?
- How is the food prepared (baked, broiled or fried)?
- Will you serve the sauce on the side?
- What kind of sauce is it?
- Will the chef honor special requests?
- Is it possible to substitute?
- Do you have low-calorie salad dressing?
- Do you have skim or nonfat milk?

Ask for plain or flavored vinegar, lemon wedges, or anything else you use at home to enhance the flavor of your food. Read the menu carefully and watch out for terms that indicate high-fat preparation, such as "crispy," "creamed," "fried," "buttered," "au gratin," "escalloped," or "sauced." Better choices are descriptors like "poached," "steamed," "roasted," "broiled," and "in its own juice."

When you order a sandwich, I cannot overemphasize how important it is for you to ask for mustard or for mayonnaise on the side. If you add the mayonnaise yourself you are in control of how much you will get. Doesn't it make much more sense for you to decide how much mayonnaise you want to eat, rather than letting the person in the kitchen who prepares the sandwiches make that decision for you? The same thing applies to a salad. If you order the salad dressing on the side, you are in control of how much of it you eat.

It always amazes me that people who wouldn't dream of letting a used-car salesman tell them what kind of car to drive, do not hesitate to let a restaurant chef or server tell them how much fat to eat. Many times people say they do not want to offend the chef or server. I ask you, why not? You insist on the quality you are paying for in a store without any qualms about offending the manager; why not do the same in a restaurant?

Be a Savvy Customer!

Make the effort to learn how different types of food preparation can affect nutrient values. You do not need the skills of a master chef to figure out that frying adds lots of calories to food and that sauces made from butter and eggs can turn a low-calorie item into a high-calorie entrée. For example: 2 ounces of steamed clams with lemon contain 60 calories, less than a gram of fat; 2 ounces of deep-fried clams contain 250 calories and 13 grams of fat. Deep-fried clams also contain about 15 grams of carbohydrate, which will have a direct impact on your blood glucose. I am not saying you cannot eat fried clams; what I am saying is as an informed consumer, know the difference between the fried and steamed clams and make a choice. If you choose the fried clams, you are choosing to eat the equivalent of $2\frac{1}{2}$ teaspoons of butter or margarine and one slice of bread with the clams. If you choose the steamed clams you can spend your fat and bread calories on other foods. The choice is yours!

Steak is another example, as ounce for ounce a T-bone steak has about 20 calories and 2 grams of fat more per ounce than a trimmed loin steak. If you have a 6-ounce steak, the cut you select can make a difference of 120 calories and about 12 grams of fat. If you do order steak, be sure to ask if the chef adds butter or oil when he broils it, and if so, request that it be broiled "dry." Added butter adds nothing but excess calories.

Chicken breast offers even greater choice, as a 6-ounce skinless serving broiled has approximately 280 calories and 6 grams of fat. Leave the skin on, dip it in batter, and deep-fry the chicken breast and it yields over 600 calories, 25 grams of fat, and 25 grams of carbohydrate! When you batter a food, like chicken or shrimp, you add flour, bread, or cracker crumbs or cornmeal, all primarily carbohydrates, so you need to consider the carbohydrate as well as the fat if you make this choice.

Clam chowder is not all the same. If you select the New England (cream) variety, 8 ounces will give you 200 calories compared to Manhattan (red), which gives you a mere 80 calories. Lobster newburg contains almost 500 calories, 27 grams of fat and 13 grams of carbohydrate in an 8-ounce serving. Four ounces of lobster meat, on the other hand, weigh in at 110 calories and less than 1 gram of fat. If you dip the lobster in butter you need to consider the calories in the butter you add. If you enhance your lobster by squeezing fresh lemon juice on it additional calories are insignificant.

You must take control in the restaurant if you wish to eat out and control your blood glucose. This is possible and can be gratifying if you are up to the challenge. **You can follow your meal plan in a restaurant!**

How familiar are you with the nutrient content of the foods you like to eat? All food fits into the categories of carbohydrates, proteins or meats, and fats, so in a restaurant you can choose accordingly.

One strategy you might try in a restaurant is to order an entrée that takes a lot of time to consume. Crab legs are a perfect example, as you have to crack them and dig the crabmeat out of the shell. If you eat one pound of king crab legs with lemon you are eating 130 calories' worth of crab, and if you dip the crab in one tablespoon of butter you double the calories. However your dinner partner who chooses fish and chips and eats the whole thing has eaten over 600 calories. Most people tend to eat less if they eat more slowly. In this situation a dinner salad, crab legs, and a roll offer a viable dinner alternative to deep-fried fish and french fries.

Try ordering à la carte (off the menu). Some people may say that it costs more to order this way, but you need to look at your priorities and ask yourself whether you can "afford" the calories in the all-inclusive dinner. If you think about the calories you have to spend in a day as carefully as you think about how you spend your money, you will probably make more healthful choices both in restaurants and at home. If you order à la carte, you might have a bowl of soup and a salad for your whole meal. Or you may order an appetizer for your entrée, then add a vegetable and a salad to complete your meal. You will not necessarily save any money, but if you are improving your health, you are making the most "economical" choice in the long run. Ordering à la carte may be the easiest way to stick with your meal plan. For example if your meal plan calls for 2 servings of starchy food, 3 ounces of meat or protein, 1 or 2 vegetables,

2 teaspoons of fat, and a serving of fruit what could you order in a restaurant?

How about a cup of chicken noodle soup, a green salad with a teaspoon of olive oil and herb vinegar, a large shrimp cocktail with 2 ounces of cocktail sauce, a side of fresh asparagus with a teaspoon of butter, and 6 saltine crackers? I will break this down so that you understand exactly how to figure it out.

2 starches:	8 ounces broth-based soup
	6 saltines
3 meat:	6 large boiled shrimp
2 vegetable:	green salad
	asparagus
2 fat:	1 teaspoon olive oil
	1 teaspoon butter
1 fruit:	2 ounces cocktail sauce

I know that cocktail sauce is not fruit, but I also know that 2 ounces of cocktail sauce contain approximately 15 grams of carbohydrate, the same amount you will find in a serving of fruit. So I know that I can substitute the carbohydrate from the cocktail sauce for the carbohydrate I would normally get from the fruit I would eat at dinner and not adversely affect my blood glucose control. This is what I mean by how well do you know your meal plan and how much do you know about the other foods you enjoy eating. Knowledge is power, and nowhere is that truer than knowledge about the food you eat.

Another example of what you might order following the same meal plan outlined above is a cup of vegetable soup, tossed salad with reduced-calorie ranch dressing, filet mignon, baked potato with two tablespoons of sour cream, steamed broccoli, fresh fruit cup for dessert, and a doggie bag. In both of these meals you need to select a calorie-free beverage. Order the doggie bag at the start of the meal and put the portion of steak and potato you want to take home in it before you start to eat. That way you will not be tempted to have just one more bite! If you ordered an 8-ounce filet, the restaurant will serve you a 6-ounce portion of cooked meat. That is because all the weights you see for meat on the menu refer to raw weight. Meat shrinks about 25 percent when it is cooked, so 8 ounces raw will shrink to 6 ounces cooked. Since our meal plan calls for a three-ounce serving, all you have to do is cut the steak in half and you have the exact amount you want to eat. The potato is a little trickier, as you need to judge how much to eat. You want one-half of an average baked potato; however, many restaurants serve giant baked potatoes. If you have been weighing and measuring at home, it will be much easier for you to estimate an appropriate serving size. Now that you have the right amount of food on your plate, let's break it down to see how it fits into your meal plan.

2 starches:	8 ounces vegetable soup
	small potato
3 meat:	3 ounces filet mignon
2 vegetables:	tossed salad
	steamed broccoli
2 fats:	2 tablespoons sour cream
	2 tablespoons reduced-fat salad dressing
1 fruit:	½ cup fresh fruit

Again, the vegetable soup counts as a starch because of its total carbohydrate content. A cup of soup contains more carbohydrate and calories than a cup of a plain steamed vegetable. The more familiar you become with the nutrient content of the food you eat, the more flexibility you will have in selecting food, while still keeping your blood glucose in good control.

The reason I suggested soup for both our menus is because soup is such a satisfying food. It tends to fill you up, and when you start a meal with a cup of soup you will be more likely to select the right quantity of the rest of the food you eat. But if you need to limit your sodium intake, this is not a good selection for you. Most restaurant and commercially prepared soups have a high sodium content.

Think ahead and ask for all your special requests when you place your order. Ask your server if these special requests are possible. If she says yes, she has committed to honoring them. Make yourself clear and be very specific in your requests as you cannot expect the server to be able to read your mind. With a lot of knowledge and a little planning you will soon become an expert at ordering and getting exactly what you want in a restaurant.

Fat City?

Earlier in this book we discussed the fact that fat is the most concentrated source of calories. It has over twice as many calories as either carbohydrate or protein in each gram. One of the reasons restaurant food is typically high in fat is because it takes just a little bit of fat to add a lot of calories and it takes a lot of vigilance to keep fat to a minimum. We know that fat adds flavor to food, which is one reason why chefs use it liberally in preparation. It takes a lot of time and effort to replace fat with other seasonings to make the food taste the same. Fat also acts as a lubricant because it keeps food from sticking to the pan, so if the chef does not want the food to stick he may use fat with a free hand. In many restaurants food is prepared in quantity, rather than to order, and food with a higher fat content will maintain its quality for a longer period of time, as the fat keeps food from drying out.

In other cases it may merely be force of habit that influences the amount of fat added to the food. Frequently, when you order broiled or grilled salmon the chef will coat it with oil prior to cooking "to keep it from sticking to the grill." Salmon is a fatty fish to begin with, and if it is cooked slowly the fat it contains will lubricate the grill, so adding additional fat is unnecessary. Herring, trout, Pacific shark, and salmon are all naturally high in fat, so if you order them request that they be broiled "dry." Most restaurants do not like to do this, as it makes it more difficult to cook the fish. A very light fish like sole or flounder may require the addition of fat to keep it from sticking. If you know the difference you can request no added fat or a minimal amount of fat added to your food. Be vigilant, and if you are served a greasy-looking fish, send it back!

Many restaurant chains have tried low-fat items and removed them from the menu because they did not sell. McDonald's McLean Deluxe is the classic example. The only way lower fat food will sell is if consumers develop a liking for it and demand these items.

Truth in Menus?

Restaurants must follow the "truth in menu" law, so you really should be able to believe what they say. As of May 2, 1997, if a restaurant menu makes any health claims about food they must comply with the Nutrition Labeling and Education Act of 1990. That was the law that mandated Nutrition Facts labeling on foods in grocery stores. So if a menu claims an item is "reduced-calorie" or "low-fat" you should be able to believe it. You do need to make the effort necessary to know what those claims mean. For example, "reduced-calorie" means that a food must contain 25 percent fewer calories than the standard item. If a serving of lasagna typically contains 400 calories, a restaurant could advertise a reduced-calorie lasagna if it provides 300 or fewer calories.

In order to advertise an item as "low-fat" it can contain only 3 grams of fat or less in a serving that is larger than 2 tablespoons or 30 grams (30 grams is just a fraction over an ounce). If a main dish or whole meal is advertised as "low-fat" it cannot have more than 3 grams of fat in a 100-gram serving and no more than 30 percent of the total calories can come from fat.

"Light" or "lite" will also have a new meaning. Items with this label must get no more than half their calories from fat or have 50 percent less fat or 33 percent fewer calories than a standard recipe. If a regular salad dressing contains 90 calories and 9 grams of fat in a tablespoon, a "light" version of the salad dressing could have no more than 60 calories and 4½ grams of fat.

Any restaurant that makes health claims must have backup for those claims, such as a computer analysis of the recipe or a cookbook version that lists values for calories, fat, saturated fat, cholesterol, and sodium. They must be able to provide their customers with this information if it is requested. If you have any doubts about what you see on the menu or on your plate, do not hesitate to ask for the nutrient information on these advertised items.

The law is strict and some restaurants will avoid anything on the menu that implies a health claim. However, many restaurants do say they are happy to honor special requests.

What about Sharing?

Like any business, restaurants must make money if they want to stay in business. A good restaurateur knows how many seats his restaurant has, how many times those seats turn over in a day, and what his profit margin is per customer. If you patronize an establishment they expect to realize a profit on your visit to help them achieve a positive bottom line. If you occupy a table the restaurant owner expects a certain amount of business. If you share an entrée with your dinner partner you are cutting the calories you eat in half, but you are also cutting into the restaurant owner's profit. Many restaurants charge a "plate" fee to help recover this loss. Other restaurants have a minimum charge per customer. It is a good idea to inquire what the policy is when you make your reservations. However, if you are concerned about your blood glucose control and your health, the "extra plate" charge may be the best choice for you.

Think Like a Celebrity!

When the rich and famous go to a restaurant they have no qualms about specifying exactly what they want and how they want it prepared. The establishment caters to their every wish. To a certain degree this is because they expect celebrity treatment. You can develop the same response merely by expecting it. You do not have to apologize because you want something special.

If in your own mind you believe that you should be able to get what you request, you will be able to do so. Be ever so courteous as you plan ahead and ask for what you need. If you have confidence that you can get what you want, your confidence will inspire the server to honor your every wish. Never forget that you are no less important than the most famous celebrity, as you are the customer and you are paying the bill, so it is not unreasonable to politely request what you want and refuse what you do not want.

Lastly, do not forget to tip. If a restaurant server goes out of his or her way to accommodate your special requests, reward them. If you are a regular customer the money you spend on the tip will be well worth the expenditure. It will insure prompt, accurate, and pleasant service.

You may wonder if you can really do the things that I have described in this chapter. Let me assure you that these techniques work. My husband and I practice them regularly and have for over 20 years, so I encourage you to profit from our experience and enjoy dining in restaurants the way you like.

Many people who eat out a lot sometimes wonder if they are getting all the vitamins they need. Are you one of them? Discover the facts about vitamins in chapter 11.

Eat Your Vitamins and Other Helpful Substances

Nutraceutical is a new word you will not find in the dictionary, at least not yet, but it can be defined the same way we do *pharmaceutical*. Pharmaceutical is the use of a drug, presumably to cure a disease, while a nutraceutical is the use of a nutrient for the same purpose.

Phytochemical is another word we are hearing a lot about these days. *Phyto* is the Greek word for *plant*, so phytochemicals are plant chemicals. They do not come from a chemistry lab but are natural compounds in plants that may have properties that prevent or cure disease.

Functional foods is yet another way to describe the same concept, as these foods have biologically active compounds that affect your health. These foods appear to offer more than just basic nutrition. The experts do not agree on an exact definition of these terms, and for the time being they are being used interchangeably.

If you recall, an earlier chapter talked about health claims on food labels, and some of the original claims referred to fruits, vegetables, and fiber as having the potential to help lower our risk for cancer and coronary heart disease. The substances in the fruits, vegetables, and fiber that are responsible for the lower risk are what are called phytochemicals, nutraceuticals, or the functional qualities of foods.

While we have experienced the benefits of these phytochemicals since the beginning of time, it is only in the twentieth century that scientists have identified these substances. Today we know that scurvy is a disease resulting from a deficiency of vitamin C in the diet. British sailors three hundred years ago learned this from experience. Vitamin C had not yet been isolated or named, but experience taught the sailors that if they ate limes during long voyages they did not develop scurvy. They ate the limes, stayed healthy, and earned the nickname Limey. To this day British sailors are known as Limeys. Vitamin C was the phytochemical that had the protective qualities for the British Navy. It is the same phytochemical or nutraceutical that you and I eat every day.

Fruits, vegetables, grains, spices, nuts, beans, seeds, and even tea have phytochemicals. As a matter of fact if you have your tea with lemon you get limonoids with your catechins! If you make a primavera sauce for pasta with tomatoes, garlic, onion, broccoli, and carrots you will eat lycopene, allicin, flavonoids, sulforaphane, and beta-carotene. Like nutraceuticals some of these phytochemical names have not yet hit the dictionary, but I am quite sure you had no idea all those strange-sounding things could taste so good!

There are thousands of other substances in food that have not been identified as yet. A 1950 edition of the *U.S. Department of Agriculture (USDA) Handbook 8 on the Composition of Foods—Raw, Processed, Prepared* includes data on vitamins A and C, thiamine, riboflavin, and niacin. Minerals listed are calcium, phosphorus, and iron. The introductory section states that "methods of extraction and assay for the three B vitamins (thiamine, riboflavin, niacin) included in these tables are still in the process of development." In 1950 only 8 vitamins and minerals were listed, reflecting the knowledge at the time. A half century later our method of extraction and assay has improved considerably and the number of known individual nutrients has expanded substantially. Just think of the potential for identifying additional nutrients over the next half century. The lesson to be learned from all of this is that the substances in food that have a protective effect were there before they were identified. There are lots of protective substances in food that have not been identified yet, but they are in the food doing their job, just as the vitamin C in the limes did for the British Navy.

Vitamins and Diabetes

Virtually every claim we hear about vitamins and disease refers to preventing cancer or heart disease. These same recommendations apply to people with diabetes and the population at large. However people with diabetes should be aware of some special considerations about chromium and magnesium.

We know that chromium deficiency is associated with elevated blood glucose, cholesterol, and triglycerides. Chromium is a part of the glucose tolerance factor, which helps us make glucose from carbohydrate in the body. It is estimated that we need between 50 and 200 micrograms of chromium each day, but most of us eat only about 25 micrograms as a part of our daily diet. We are starting to see more research on the effect of chromium supplementation. Check with your health care provider to see if you should take chromium, and if so at what dosage.

Magnesium is another mineral that affects your glucose tolerance. If you are an average American you may be getting less than you need. One of the symptoms of too much magnesium is chronic diarrhea, so you do not want to overdo it. The experts recommend that men get 350 milligrams and women 280 milligrams daily. Many common over-the-counter medications contain magnesium: Bayer Plus, Bufferin, Di-Gel, Maalox, Mylanta, and Phillips' Milk of Magnesia all contain magnesium. If you have impaired kidney problems consult your physician before taking any over-the-counter medications.

Antioxidants

An antioxidant is a compound found in food that may protect against cancer and other diseases by neutralizing unstable molecules found in the body that are called free radicals. Free radicals work in your body in a fashion similar to the way that moisture and air work on unprotected metal. Look at an old car that has been exposed to all kinds of weather—it is rusty. The process that causes rust is called oxidation.

Environmental influences like smoke, sunlight, and smog cause free radicals to develop in your body, and it is believed that these contribute to the development of degenerative diseases like heart disease, cancers, and respiratory problems. Antioxidants can bind with the free radicals in your body, rendering them harmless.

Beta-carotene, vitamin C, and vitamin E are all antioxidants. Any food that is a good source of these substances is also a good source of antioxidants. Carrots, kiwi fruit, and peanut butter are antioxidant foods.

Prominent researchers around the world are also conducting major studies on antioxidant supplements to see if they work. Finnish researchers studied the effects of beta-carotene supplements on 30,000 men who smoked. When they began their research they were quite sure that they would prove that supplementing with beta-carotene would reduce the risk for lung cancer and death in these smokers. Wrong! The smokers who were taking the pill form of beta-carotene were not developing less cancer than the group that was taking the placebo; in fact, they actually had a higher incidence of lung cancer.

About the same time another study was being conducted in the United States funded by the National Cancer Institute. This study looked at 18,000 men and women at high risk for lung cancer because of a history of cigarette smoking or occupational exposure to asbestos. Experts ended this study in 1996, almost 2 years early, because the evidence showed that the people taking supplements (beta-carotene and vitamin A) had a higher, not lower, risk of cancer and heart disease. Death rates were higher in this group as well.

The third study that gave the same results was the Physicians Health Study, which lasted 12 years and had 22,000 male physician participants. Half of these men took beta-carotene and the other half took a placebo. The results showed no difference in the incidence of heart disease, cancer, or total deaths between the two groups. That means the beta-carotene supplement had no effect. It didn't hurt and it didn't help.

Nevertheless, population-based evidence showed that in countries where people eat a lot of green and yellow vegetables there is a lower rate of some cancers. The researchers also found that people who ate a lot of foods containing beta-carotene had the highest blood levels of beta-carotene and a lower risk of cancer. The evidence shows that beta-carotene in food works. We cannot explain why, but it sure makes a case for eating carrots or any other vegetables that contain beta-carotene.

People who eat diets high in vitamin C appear to be at lower risk for cancer, heart disease, and cataracts. One study showed that an important difference between people with cataracts and those without appeared to be the amount of foods rich in vitamin C eaten by each group.

Evidence is growing that we need more than 60 milligrams, the recommended amount of vitamin C. Some experts are saying we need to get 200 to 400 milligrams of this antioxidant each day. That is fairly easy to do if you eat five servings of fruits and vegetables each day. Adding a supplement may provide you with extra benefits, but remember to add it to your five servings of fruits and vegetables rather than use it to replace them. Supplemental vitamin C taken at the first sign of a cold may reduce the symptoms; however, at this time the research does not show that vitamin C supplements prevent colds.

Food Sources of Beta-Carotene and Vitamin C*

Food	Amount	Calories	Carbo-hydrate (grams)	Beta-carotene (ug)	Vitamin C (mg)
Kiwi fruit	1	46	11	14	75
Orange	1	62	15	28	70
Cantaloupe	1 cup	56	14	515	68
Broccoli	1 cup	25	6	136	82
Carrot	1 whole	31	8	2025	7
Red pepper	1 whole	20	5	421	140
Spinach	1 cup, raw	7	2	201	8
Squash	½ cup	40	10	365	10
Tomato	1	26	6	76	24

*Information from USDA Nutrient Database for Standard Reference
Note: ug = micrograms, mg = milligrams, g = grams

It is easy to see that though a carrot is the best source of beta-carotene listed, it is also readily apparent that eating a variety of fruits and vegetables will supply adequate amounts of both beta-carotene and vitamin C with the added bonus of fiber for very few calories. Fruits and vegetables really are nutrient bargains!

What about vitamin E? The best food sources of vitamin E are soybean oil, corn oil, hazelnuts, sunflower seeds, and wheat germ. Whole-grain cereals and eggs also provide some. Most of us do not eat enough of these foods to get all the vitamin E we need. The official recommended amount is 30 IU (international units) a day. Some experts recommend we get between 100 and 400 IU daily. The research shows that taking that amount helps decrease the risk of heart disease and some cancers as well as reduce the risk for developing cataracts. Vitamin E supplements appear to be safe, but if you take any anticlotting drugs, check with your doctor before taking this supplement.

Other Healthful Foods

Broccoli and other cruciferous vegetables: Broccoli is the vegetable George Bush made famous when he was president, going on national television saying he hated it. If you, like one of our former presidents, hate broccoli, check the rest of the cruciferous vegetables and eat the ones you like. Other cruciferous vegetables include brussels sprouts, cabbage, cauliflower, kale, mustard greens, turnips, and watercress. This family of vegetables contains isothiocyanates, which have an anticarcinogenic effect. These vegetables are delicious steamed, but do not overcook them, as their flavors will become strong and they will look mushy and unappetizing.

Enjoy Your Vitamins

Citrus peel: By now you are familiar with the benefits of citrus fruit, but did you know that the peel of the fruit also contains phytochemicals? Limonoids are found in citrus oils that we get from the rind of lemons, limes, oranges, grapefruits, and other citrus fruits. They are being studied to determine their role in the prevention of breast cancer. Every time you grate the rind of citrus fruit and include it in a recipe or squeeze lemon and drop the wedge into tea you are adding limonoids to your diet.

Garlic: Garlic has traditionally been considered to have magical powers. The movies portray its legendary ability to repel vampires. It appears that allicin, the phytochemical in garlic that gives it its strong taste and odor and also re-pelled the vampires, is also credited with the ability to help reduce the risk for heart disease and some cancers. As little as ½ clove of garlic a day is reputed to lower cholesterol and blood pressure. The downside, of course, is that the characteristic odor lingers and may repel friends and your spouse as well. To counteract this effect, try eating some *fresh parsley after you eat garlic.* This garnish, which most people think of as being merely decorative, is a natural breath freshener and may aid in digestion. Fresh parsley is also a good source of vitamins A and C, folate, and iron.

Grapes: For several years the popular press has sung the praises of red wine and its role in explaining the French paradox. The French paradox is that they eat more butter and lard and have higher cholesterol and blood pressure than Americans; however, Americans have a higher death rate due to coronary heart disease than the French. When the researchers looked at other differences in diet they learned that the French drink more red wine and also eat more fruits and vegetables than people in this country. Red wine is thought to be what made the difference. Anthocyanins, the phytochemicals believed to be responsible for this, are also found in grape juice, so you can get the benefits without the alcohol, if you wish. Resveratrol, another substance found in grapes, may help prevent some cancers. *Before you fill your glass too full with either grape juice or red wine, remember the old adage "moderation in all things," and be sure to take into account the effect these beverages have on your blood glucose.*

Soybeans: Soy products contain phytochemicals called isoflavones or phytoestrogen. The isoflavone called genistein appears to lower cholesterol and along with daidzein may reduce your risk of osteoporosis. Research is under way to test the effect of soy products on menopause and cancer.

Some of the soy products that we find in the grocery or specialty store include tofu, soy milk, textured vegetable protein products, soy flour, miso (a condiment), and edamame, which are soybeans eaten as a green vegetable. While more research is needed to pinpoint specifics, you can't go wrong including more soy products in your diet.

Tea: If you do not count water, tea is the most common beverage consumed throughout the world, and we are learning that it may offer more than a morning or afternoon lift. Tea contains a flavonoid called quercetin, which may help prevent heart disease, and a polyphenol called catechin that may help protect against stomach cancer. Isn't it great that this soothing, refreshing beverage that we enjoy either hot or iced has so many potential benefits? On top of everything else it is calorie-free!

Tomatoes: Lycopene is the name of the substance in ripe tomatoes that gives them their red color, but it appears to do much more than make tomatoes look and taste good. Lycopene content is higher in canned tomato products such as tomato paste, sauce, and ketchup than it is in raw tomatoes because processing concentrates lycopene. Studies show that this antioxidant protects against prostate cancer and may have a positive effect on the general ability of elderly people to function. But do not abandon raw tomatoes for the processed variety, as another study indicates that people who eat 7 or more servings of raw tomatoes a week reduced their risk for developing colon, rectal, stomach, and other digestive tract cancers. The experts agree that we need additional research to discover more about the properties of the tomato. In the meantime enjoy it in all of its forms.

The **bottom line** is that research into what substances in foods protect against disease is still in its infancy. From a scientific perspective, we have barely scratched the tip of the iceberg in our knowledge of the protective benefits of vegetables and fruits. There is mounting evidence of the benefits of specific nutrients found in some foods such as beta-carotene and lycopene. More important, I have never seen any reports of negative effects of eating vegetables and fruits as part of a healthful diet. As of now the experts are not completely clear about what provides the protective effect, whether it is a single nutrient or a combination of different things, so the best advice is to include and enjoy a wide variety of vegetables and fruits in your diet.

Vitamin Supplements

By now it should be pretty apparent to you that just taking a vitamin pill and not making good food choices just will not work. There is strong research and epidemiological data to show that people who eat diets high in fruits and vegetables cut their risk of developing cancer and heart disease. This is particularly important for people with diabetes, because if you already have diabetes you want to do your best to avoid any other disease.

The USDA recommends that we eat 5 to 9 servings of fruits and vegetables each day. But the question remains: is it enough? Should you still take a supplement? There is some research that says yes to this question. As we age, we tend to have a reduced immune response, so it may be a good idea to check with your physician about taking a multivitamin with minerals to correct any deficiencies. Do not overdo; too much of a good thing can cause harm, and remember that a pill can only supplement, not replace, a healthful diet.

If you take medication for your diabetes, whether it be pills or insulin, there is a lot you should know about how foods work with your medication. Learn what you need to know in chapter 12.

Balancing Food and Medication

Some people who have type 2 diabetes are able to control their blood glucose by healthful eating and physical activity. Others need to add medication in order to maintain their blood glucose in the proper range. Medications include insulin and several different types of pills or oral medications that can help keep blood glucose under control.

Insulin

The discovery of insulin in 1921 revolutionized diabetes treatment. Prior to that time the only treatment for people with diabetes whose pancreas did not produce insulin was starvation. Calories were severely restricted and the small amount of food these people were able to eat consisted primarily of fat. After insulin was discovered the diagnosis of diabetes was no longer an immediate death sentence. But from that time forward the importance of balancing food with in-

Balance Medication and Food

sulin became apparent. For years people who required insulin to control their diabetes were tied to rigid eating schedules. Fortunately, there have been many advances in insulin and now flexibility is the watchword of the day.

The reason insulin does not come in a pill form is that it is an amino acid chain and like any protein will break down during digestion. Then you would have individual amino acids rather than insulin.

If the thought of injecting insulin is frightening to you, you are not alone. No one enjoys giving themselves an injection. Just as there have been major advances in both oral medications and insulin, there have been big improvements in insulin syringes. Needles and syringes are now disposable and do not have to be sharpened or sterilized. The needles are smaller and shorter and not nearly so frightening. We have insulin pens and other delivery devices to make injecting insulin easier.

The most important thing to remember is your own overall health and well-being. If your pancreas cannot produce the insulin you need, it is time to start insulin therapy. People will often put off starting insulin because they think they just cannot give themselves injections or they think that if they start insulin they have really serious diabetes.

When they finally begin to take insulin they find they feel better than they have in a long time, because they are getting appropriate treatment.

All insulin is not the same. For years, we got insulin from the pancreases of cows and pigs. Today the source of insulin is either animal or synthetically produced human insulin. However, these days most doctors usually will start all patients on the synthetically produced human insulin. It is important to remember that when you inject insulin you are trying to do the same thing your pancreas does. That is, provide the right amount of insulin at the right time so that you can use the glucose that your body makes from the food you eat to provide the energy you need for your daily activities.

Different kinds of insulins have different actions and are classified as short-, intermediate-, and long-acting. Your doctor can prescribe combinations of these insulins to try to mimic the action of the pancreas. You can compare insulin to driving a car. With an automatic transmission, your automobile shifts from one gear to another in response to your foot on the gas pedal or brake and you do not even think about how this happens. If you have a manual transmission, you must shift gears in response to your foot on the accelerator or brake. Even with a manual transmission, your response becomes automatic over time. You shift gears without even thinking about it. But remember back to when you were first learning to drive. If you did not shift at the right moment the car stalled. When a person with diabetes requires insulin to manage their blood glucose, their pancreas has shifted from automatic to manual. Just as you learned to drive a car, you can also learn how to manage your blood glucose. Before you developed diabetes your pancreas made insulin in response to the food you ate. Now you inject insulin in anticipation of the amount of food you will eat. Once you have injected the insulin you do not have any control over its action, so it is important to match meals and snacks to the action of the insulin. Remember, once you have injected the insulin it keeps on working, whether you eat or do not eat, so you must be concerned with the "timing" of medication and food.

The most important thing you need to understand is the action of insulin. There are three things to know about the action of insulin and they are the onset, the peak, and the duration of the insulin. In other words, after you inject insulin you want to determine when it starts to act (the onset), when it is most effective (peak), and how long it lasts (duration). This is important because if you inject insulin you need to eat so that glucose is available in the bloodstream at the same time that the insulin is reaching its peak of action. If insulin peaks and you have not eaten, your blood glucose will drop and you will have a hypoglycemic reaction. Information on how to treat a hypoglycemic reaction is discussed at the end of this chapter.

Different types of insulin act for different lengths of time. Human insulin acts more quickly and does not last as long as animal insulin. The following chart shows the differences in action of the different types of insulin.

Animal Insulin Action

Type	Onset (hours)	Peak (hours)	Duration (hours)
Short-acting	½ to 2	3 to 4	4 to 6
Intermediate-acting (NPH or Lente)	4 to 6	8 to 14	16 to 20
Long-acting (Ultralente)	8 to 14	Minimal	24 to 36

Human Insulin Action

Type	Onset (hours)	Peak (hours)	Duration (hours)
Short-acting	½ to 1	2 to 3	3 to 6
Intermediate-acting (NPH or Lente)	2 to 4	4 to 12	10 to 18
Long-acting (Ultralente)	6 to 10	No detectable peak	18 to 20

Short-acting insulin can also be called regular insulin; intermediate-acting insulin is known as NPH or Lente; and long-acting is known as Ultralente insulin. Short-acting insulin is a clear liquid and intermediate- and long-acting insulins are cloudy in appearance.

If you need insulin to control your blood glucose your physician and other members of their health care team will help you work out a schedule of when and how much insulin to take for the food you eat to keep everything in balance. Most people take more than one kind of insulin, and the different-acting insulins can be mixed to get the most effective dose. The companies that manufacture insulin are making premixed insulin available, even in the very convenient insulin pens. Premixed varieties available in the United States are 70/30 and 50/50 insulins.

It may seem that if you inject insulin, you lose a lot of flexibility about when you could eat, but that is not necessarily true. If you inject insulin it is necessary to eat in response to the action of that insulin. For example, if you took intermediate-acting insulin at breakfast, you would probably need to eat a midafternoon snack to prevent the development of hypoglycemia because the intermediate-acting insulin would peak in the middle of the afternoon.

That is the reason why people who take insulin are usually advised to eat 3 meals and 2 or 3 snacks a day.

In 1996, Eli Lilly and Company introduced a very-fast-acting insulin analog called lispro insulin (Humalog). This insulin has some real advantages, as it begins to act within 5 minutes of being injected. You take it immediately before a meal. The company's recommendation is to dose and eat, and there should not be a wait at all. So if you are at a restaurant or party and your meal is delayed, all you need to do is wait until the meal is ready before you take your insulin. With lispro insulin, you can eliminate the danger of premeal hypoglycemia if the meal is delayed, making it easier to live in the real world.

Novo Nordisk has submitted its insulin analog, aspart (Novolog), to the FDA and is awaiting approval as this book goes to press.

Insulin Analog Action

Type	Onset (minutes)	Peak (hours)	Duration (hours)
Lispro	5 to 15	1 to 1½	2

The danger of hypoglycemia between meals is very small because these very-fast-acting insulins act when you need them and do not carry over to the between-meal period when you do not need them. This is an important fact for people who may need to lose weight, because overtreatment of hypoglycemia causes weight gain.

If you take regular insulin 30 minutes before a meal it begins to act at the same time you begin to eat. The regular insulin will peak or be most effective in lowering your blood glucose between 2 and 4 hours after you eat. Even though you are eating an adequate quantity of food at your meals for good nutrition, you may have to eat something between meals when your insulin peaks to prevent or treat hypoglycemia. Those "extra" calories contribute to extra weight. If you take lispro insulin you can avoid that post-meal hypoglycemia and the need to consume calories for treatment.

Ideally when the doctor prescribes insulin for a person with diabetes the goal is to mimic the action of the healthy pancreas. The usual insulin regimen is a combination of an intermediate- or long-acting insulin with a fast-or very-fast-acting insulin. The longer-acting insulin provides what is called basal coverage and the faster-acting insulin provides the amount needed to cover the food eaten at a specific meal. It is almost impossible for a person to achieve good blood glucose control with one injection a day. Many people take two or three injections a day in order to get good blood glucose control and also some flexibility in their eating schedule.

It is important for anyone who injects insulin to always carry an antidote to treat hypoglycemia. There are commercial preparations on the market that work well, and you can also use Life Savers or sugar packets, which are just as portable. The important issue is to always be prepared.

Oral Diabetes Medications

If your pancreas is still producing insulin but it does not react quickly enough in response to the food eaten at a meal, it may be time to try a medication that would help your pancreas produce more insulin. If your body is producing enough insulin, but you are unable to use it efficiently, there is another type of medication that may help. If your liver is working overtime making glucose, there is still another type of pill. There is even a medication that can slow down the absorption of carbohydrate in the small intestine. Some people with type 2 diabetes need to take insulin to keep their blood glucose in an acceptable range while others can use the oral medications. The important thing to remember is that if you are taking any medication you need to understand how it affects your body and what precautions must be taken to minimize any side effects.

To keep your blood glucose under control it is important that you have an adequate supply of insulin in your body at the right time so that it can work in conjunction with the food you eat. If you take a pill that enhances insulin action or inject insulin and do not eat you may be putting yourself at risk for hypoglycemia or low blood glucose. So it is very important that you know how the medication you are taking really works.

There are five different kinds or classes of oral medications used to treat diabetes. These pills all act at different places in the body. They attack the blood glucose problem in many different ways. If you think about diabetes and its effect on the body, the action of these varied medications will make more sense.

Diabetes is diagnosed by measuring blood glucose. We need insulin so that the glucose from the food can get into the cells. Different types of oral medications act at specific sites in the body to keep the blood glucose in the ideal range. The pancreas makes insulin and the liver manufactures glucose. The intestines break the food down into glucose. The cells then use glucose for energy.

Oral Diabetes Medications

Class	Action	Generic Name	Brand Name
Sulfonyl-ureas	Stimulate the pancreas to produce insulin.	tolbutamide tolazamide chlorpropamide glipizide glyburide glimepiride	Orinase Tolinase Diabinese Glucotrol Glucotrol XL Diabeta Micronase Glynase PresTab Amaryl
Meglitinide	Stimulates the pancreas to produce insulin in the presence of glucose.	repaglinide	Prandin
Alpha-glucosidase inhibitors	Act in the small intestine to slow down the release of glucose.	acarbose miglitol	Precose Glyset
Biguanides	Act primarily in the liver, decreasing the production of glucose by the liver. Help decrease the absorption of glucose from the intestine and increase the action of insulin on the muscle tissue.	metformin	Glucophage
Thiazo-lidinediones	Changes the way the body uses insulin. Helps insulin move glucose into the cells so it can be used for energy.	rosiglitazone pioglitazone HCL	Avandia Actos

All of these drugs should be used *in addition to healthful eating and adequate physical activity*. It is important to remember that medication *does not* take the place of these healthful behaviors. Medications can be very useful in helping to control blood glucose; however, they should be used as an adjunct to, not a replacement for, a healthy lifestyle.

Sulfonylureas

There is a wide spectrum of sulfonylureas. This type of drug was the first "diabetes pill" and for many years the only type of oral medication available for people with type 2 diabetes. These drugs work in the pancreas and can only be used by people whose pancreas is producing some insulin. People who are allergic to sulfa cannot take these drugs. They are broken down in the liver so anyone with liver disease or a history of alcoholism should not take them. One of the side effects of these drugs may be weight gain. This is bad news, because most people with type 2 diabetes need to lose weight. The sulfonylureas are divided into two groups based on the length of time they have been in use. The older ones that have been around the longest are called the first-generation drugs. The newer drugs were named second-generation sulfonylureas.

The first-generation sulfonylureas are tolbutamide (Orinase), tolazamide (Tolinase), and chlorpropamide (Diabinese). These drugs are still in use but seldom prescribed for a person newly diagnosed with diabetes. Orinase is the shortest acting of these drugs and is usually taken two or three times a day, before meals. Tolinase lasts longer and is usually taken once, but in some cases twice a day. Diabinese is the longest acting drug and is only given once a day. These pills should be taken at or before the first meal of the day. If you are taking these drugs be aware that they work in your body for many hours. If you skip a meal they continue to work to lower your blood glucose and consequently, it may go too low, resulting in hypoglycemia.

Two second-generation drugs have been used since the early 1980s. They are glipizide (Glucotrol and Glucotrol

XL) and glyburide (Diabeta, Micronase, and Glynase PresTab). These drugs may be taken once or twice a day and are always taken before a meal. The newest sulfonylurea drug is glimepiride, a pill with the brand name Amaryl. It should be taken at breakfast or with the first meal of the day.

You may wonder what the difference is between the first and second generations of these drugs. Some differences are that the second-generation drugs have fewer side effects, less possibility of interacting with other drugs, and increased effectiveness. Since all the second-generation drugs are active for approximately 24 hours it is important that people taking these medications space their meals at regular intervals throughout the day. Any of the sulfonylurea drugs can cause hypoglycemia. It is important that you follow your doctor's advice on the dosage and timing of these drugs to avoid any problems. You should also be aware of the possibility of hypoglycemia and how to treat it should it occur.

Meglitinide

Repaglinide (Prandin) is a meglitinide. Repaglinide is a nonsulfonylurea insulin-releasing agent that increases the secretion of insulin from the beta cells of the pancreas. It acts very quickly and causes the pancreas to secrete insulin for only one to two hours. Taken before meals the insulin is available to control blood glucose levels after the meal. If you take this medication, it is important to eat within a half hour. If you skip a meal you should skip the medication as well. Repaglinide, like any medication that affects blood glucose, can cause hypoglycemia.

Alpha-Glucosidase Inhibitors

Acarbose (Precose) and miglitol (Glyset) are alpha-glucosidase inhibitors. These medications work in the small intestine to slow down the release of glucose from carbohydrate. They help prevent the digestion of starch and some other carbohydrates in the first part of the small intestine and consequently slow the absorption of glucose. These medications need to be taken with the very first bite of food, at the beginning of the meal. This is because they work in the first section of the small intestine, and in order to work properly the medication and the food need to be in the small intestine at the same time.

These drugs do not affect the digestion of simple sugars that are also called monosaccharides. That means that these drugs work on starches and disaccharides, foods that take more steps to digest, such as breads, cereals, grain products, vegetables, beans, and table sugar. They do not affect the digestion of foods whose carbohydrate is mostly simple sugar such as milk, yogurt, honey, corn syrup, most fruits, and commercial products designed to treat hypoglycemia.

The most common side effects are flatulence (gas), abdominal pain, and diarrhea. That is why your doctor will start you with a small dose of one of these drugs and slowly increase the dosage as tolerated. It is best to avoid "gasforming" foods, especially when first starting on these drugs, until your body has a chance to adapt. Foods like dried beans, cabbage, and broccoli fall in this category. It is important that these particular drugs be started slowly and that the dosage be increased gradually, as your body needs time to adjust to the medication. People who have inflammatory bowel disease, colon ulcers, or other intestinal problems should not use these drugs.

You may wonder if alpha-glucosidase inhibitors can cause hypoglycemia. If they interfere with the digestion of some sugars and starches, would they interfere with treating a hypoglycemic reaction? Acarbose and miglitol do not increase the production of insulin by the pancreas, so they do not cause hypoglycemia. However, many people take acarbose or miglitol and a sulfonylurea. People on that regimen do need to think about treating potential hypoglycemia.

The two important things to remember are that alpha-glucosidase inhibitors are effective in the first part of the small intestine and do not stay in this section very long. If you take these medications with the first bite of food, they will travel out of the intestine with the food. Low blood glucose reactions occur before you eat, not after. So if and when you have a reaction there will probably not be any alpha-glucosidase inhibitor in the first section of your small intestine. Second, if you do have a hypoglycemic reaction, treat it with a food or product that is not affected by an alpha-glucosidase inhibitor. Milk, yogurt, fruit, honey, or corn syrup are foods that will work; table sugar will not. Another alternative is to treat your reaction with a commercially prepared product. There are a variety of glucose gels and tablets you can purchase that are specifically designed to treat low-blood-glucose reactions. The benefits of a commercial preparation are that it is easy to take the correct amount of carbohydrate and they are convenient to carry in your purse or pocket. Because they are a treatment rather than a treat, people tend to use them correctly.

Biguanide

Metformin (Glucophage) is a biguanide. Metformin acts primarily on the liver. One of the functions of the liver is to keep our blood glucose at the proper level. If it senses that the cells need glucose it can make glucose to supply the cells. When you develop diabetes this mechanism gets out of balance and the liver may produce more glucose than you need. Metformin helps control blood glucose by decreasing the liver's glucose production. It helps your insulin act more effectively in transporting glucose into muscle tissue. It also helps lower LDL cholesterol levels (that is the bad kind) and triglycerides. Unlike the sulfonylureas, people taking metformin tend to lose weight or stay the same weight. Most of the side effects of this drug are gastrointestinal. Diarrhea, nausea, vomiting, abdominal bloating, flatulence (gas), and anorexia (loss of appetite) are the major problems. These symptoms usually disappear over time. The symptoms also seem to be dose related. So if you start out with a small dose and gradually build up to the optimal, you may tolerate the drug better. But if symptoms persist, discuss them with your health care provider. People with kidney disease should not take this drug. The side effects are minimized if you take the drug with food, so you should take it at the beginning of the first meal of the day.

Metformin does not cause hypoglycemia. However, in many instances it may be taken in combination with a sulfonylurea. Combining these drugs may increase the action of both of them, so in these cases hypoglycemia may occur. Sometimes acarbose may be added to the combination. In that case, you would have to consider using a commercial preparation or milk to treat hypoglycemia.

Thiazolidinediones

Rosiglitazone (Avandia) and pioglitazone hydrochloride (Actos) are thiazolidinediones. They help to improve cell response to insulin. Thiazolidinediones work by helping glucose move into the cells where it can be used for energy. For this to happen, insulin must be present. Moving glucose from the blood to the cells also reduces the blood glucose. Rosiglitazone and pioglitazone HCL can be taken with or without food once or twice a day, depending on your health care providers' recommendation.

It is very important to talk to your doctor about interactions if you are taking any of these drugs. If you are seeing more than one physician, it is a good practice to get in the habit of telling each doctor about any medication another physician prescribed.

It is important to remember that many of the drugs we are talking about are very new. The FDA has only approved most of them since 1995. Though the majority of the sulfonylureas have been on the market for years, glimepiride is the exception. All of the other oral medications have been on the market in the United States for a short time. These new drugs help to improve the quality of life for people with diabetes. And this is just the beginning. Approximately 20 new diabetes drugs are currently being tested and/or are awaiting FDA approval.

Insulin and Oral Medication

Sometimes your physician may prescribe a combination of drugs. BIDS is an acronym for bedtime insulin, daytime sulfonylureas. If you have a normal blood glucose when you go to bed, and always wake up with a high fasting plasma glucose, BIDS therapy may be indicated. Intermediate-acting insulin is injected at bedtime to control blood glucose overnight, and one of the sulfonylureas is given at breakfast to control the blood glucose after meals. The other oral medications can be used in conjunction with insulin as well. It is important you work with your health care provider to get the medication regimen that will work best for you.

Whether your diabetes is type 1 or type 2, and whether or not you take insulin or pills, it is impossible to overemphasize that diabetes is a disease that needs to be taken very seriously even if you do not take any medication. Sometimes we hear people say they have "borderline" diabetes. There is no such thing. "Borderline diabetes" is like being just a little bit pregnant. The bottom line is either you have it or you don't! Complications such as retinopathy (loss of vision) and neuropathy (loss of sensation in the foot, for example) may develop in people with either type of diabetes when it is not controlled. The most important things you can do are to get good medical care and the education to learn how you can help yourself. The type of medication you take to control your diabetes (whether you take pills or inject insulin) does not make it more, or less, serious.

On the Horizon

In 1987 researchers discovered amylin, a hormone that is secreted by the pancreas that works with insulin to help control blood glucose. Until this discovery we thought two hormones, insulin and glucagon, did this job all by themselves. Now we know that amylin is produced by the beta cells and is secreted with insulin to regulate blood glucose. When a person who does not have diabetes eats a meal or snack, the beta cells in the pancreas secrete insulin and amylin to help properly metabolize that meal. Insulin helps to move glucose into the body tissues and into muscle and liver to be stored as glycogen. Amylin works to regulate the speed at which food is moved from the gut to the circulatory system by controlling the amount of glycogen the liver releases. It works hand in hand with insulin and glucagon to keep blood glucose in control.

Like insulin, amylin is missing in people with type 1 diabetes and deficient in some people with type 2 diabetes. Insulin production decreases over time in people with type 2 diabetes, and amylin production decreases in a parallel fashion.

As we go to press with this book, amylin replacement is still experimental. We hope it will soon be available to help people with diabetes.

Hypoglycemia

Hypoglycemia is a technical term for low blood glucose. If extreme, hypoglycemia will result in a loss of consciousness. It may be caused by too much medication, delayed meals, too little food, or extremely heavy exercise. If you think you may be having a hypoglycemic episode, the first thing you need to do is to check yourself to see if you really do have low blood glucose. If the number is below 70 mg/dl it is time to do something. The rule of thumb is to eat 15 grams of carbohydrate and wait 15 minutes to see if your blood glucose responds. There are products available in your pharmacy that are specifically designed to treat hypoglycemia that you should always have on hand. They are packaged and easy to carry and you can keep them in your purse, pocket, or car. The recommended dose of any of these products will automatically give you 15 grams of carbohydrate. However, you can also get 15 grams of carbohydrate from ½ cup of fruit juice or ½ cup of a soft drink sweetened with sugar, or 3 packets of sugar, or 1 tablespoon of honey or 5 or 6 Life Savers. Usually, people who take oral diabetes medication can avoid hypoglycemia merely by eating their meals at regular intervals.

Sometimes hypoglycemia can occur because you are getting too much medication. If you lose weight after starting on a sulfonylurea or insulin your body may require less medication. Or if you start an exercise program your body may use the medication more efficiently and consequently you may need a smaller dose to keep your blood glucose under control. It is very important to monitor your blood glucose and record those readings along with food eaten, exercise, and amount of medication taken. Your primary health care provider will use your records to determine if your medication needs to be adjusted.

Whatever the cause, if hypoglycemia occurs, treat it promptly. The following table lists foods and commercial products that can be used to treat hypoglycemia.

Treating Hypoglycemia

Fruit Juice	½ cup
Regular (sweetened) soda	½ cup
Table sugar	3 teaspoons or 3 packets
Honey	1 tablespoon
Life Savers	4 to 5
Dex4 glucose tabs	4 tablets
BD Glucose Tablets	3 tablets

Insta-Glucose	1 tube
Monojel	1 packet
Generic glucose tablets	See package directions

Amounts of food listed here represent approximately 15 grams of carbohydrate.

Amounts of the commercial preparations are the manufacturer's recommendations.

You may be feeling overwhelmed at this point and may want to get some help. Chapter 13 is your answer. A registered dietitian who is a Certified Diabetes Educator is an expert on all nutrition-related diabetes questions.

Finding a Dietitian

Do you need a dietitian? Absolutely! Make friends with your dietitian. He or she can teach you how to eat while maintaining good glucose control. It is just as important for people who have diabetes to have their own personal dietitian, ideally a dietitian who is also a Certified Diabetes Educator (C.D.E.), as it is they have a personal physician. Just as you see your physician periodically to make sure your overall health is okay, you should see your dietitian/C.D.E. to check that your meal plan is on track.

Why Do I Need a Dietitian?

All of us do need help from time to time, especially when it comes to making good food choices. When you decide you have done all you can on your own or that it is just time to assess where you stand or if you are concerned that you are not getting all the vitamins and minerals you need, it may be time to consult your dietitian.

Healthful eating should be a long-term goal for every-one, whether they have diabetes or not. In an age where medication is available to "fix" almost every ailment it has become very easy to think that what we eat does not count. Life would be much easier if we could just take a pill to cure diabetes and not care about food or exercise. In reality there are some people who do need medication to help keep their blood glucose in an acceptable range, but all people with diabetes need to make good food choices and live a physically active lifestyle.

Self-management is the key to good diabetes manage-ment. The most important person on the medical team is you, the person who has diabetes. Even though you have read this book, you may feel you need some additional help to achieve your goals. Your dietitian/C.D.E. can teach you how to make healthful food choices and how food affects your blood glucose. She or he can teach you how to solve problems and learn how to make food choices that will im-prove your health.

If weight loss is your goal, and it is for the greatest ma-jority of people with type 2 diabetes, food portion size and methods of preparation become very important issues. A dietitian can help you decide how many calories are rea-sonable and practical for you to eat at each meal and each day. She or he can also help you learn that what you put in your food during preparation and what you add to your food at the table will affect your blood glucose. If you have a life-time membership in the "clean plate" club *now* is the time for change, and your dietitian can help. Variety and moder-ation are the keys to healthful eating. The important thing is to consciously make food choices to promote your good health. Remember, good health and good glucose control are your goals, and when you achieve them, weight will generally take care of itself. The important thing is to consciously make food choices to promote your good health.

Where Can I Find a Dietitian?

Your physician is the first person to ask when you are looking for a dietitian. She or he may have a dietitian they work with who is knowledgeable about diabetes or better yet is also a Certified Diabetes Educator. If your physician does not make a specific recommendation, try to find a dietitian whose credentials are R.D., C.D.E. This means the person is a Registered Dietitian who is a Certified Diabetes Educator. To be able to use the initials R.D. he or she has to have had a minimum of a four-year college degree, have completed a preprofessional experience (internship), and passed an exam. This individual has in-depth knowledge about medical nutrition therapy and will be familiar with food and drug interactions and how food will affect your blood glucose. They can also help integrate your favorite foods into your diabetes meal plan and advise you on how to deal with any dietary restrictions you may have, whether they be for religious or medical reasons.

Certified Diabetes Educator (C.D.E.) is a multidisciplinary credential that affirms professionals have specialized knowledge in diabetes education. This is in addition to the first degree. So you may find C.D.E. after R.N. if a nurse is a C.D.E., or after the R.D. for a dietitian. You may even find C.D.E. after M.D., as there are about 240 physicians with this credential. In order to become a C.D.E., a professional must meet strict criteria. Every five years these professionals must show proof that they have spent a certain number of hours in face-to-face diabetes patient education. They must pass an exam that covers a basic knowledge of all aspects of diabetes in order to use the initials C.D.E. This exam is the same for everyone, whether they are a nurse, a dietitian, a pharmacist, a physician, or any other eligible health professional. The C.D.E. credential verifies direct patient contact in addition to measuring basic knowledge.

You can also find an R.D. at any American Diabetes Association Recognized Education Program. For information on locating a program in your area call 1–800–342–2383. These programs are designed to offer comprehensive self-management training for people with diabetes. These programs are usually staffed with a registered nurse and a registered dietitian who are both knowledgeable in diabetes care and education, and many times they are C.D.E.'s.

Or call the National Center for Nutrition and Dietetics at The American Dietetic Association, 1–800–366–1655. Ask for R.D.'s who are C.D.E.'s in the area where you live.

It is important to keep in mind that any health care professional can be of more assistance to you if you have a good rapport with that person, whether they be a dietitian, nurse, physician, or member of any other discipline. So if you just do not like the first dietitian you consult, do not give up. There are over 70,000 out there, and one is just right for you. With a little effort you will find the right provider who can offer you the help you need so that you can be in control.

How Often Should I See My Dietitian?

It is a good idea to visit your dietitian at least once a year. Does that sound like a revolutionary idea? It shouldn't. After all, most of us eat at least three times a day. Many Americans gain weight over their lifetime, even though the experts say that is not "healthy" or recommended. Regular visits with your dietitian can help you maintain good glucose control and a reasonable weight.

You also need to figure out if anything is going on in your life that may be affecting your blood glucose. If all of a sudden you find your belt no longer fits, it may be time to stop and look at what you are eating. If your circumstances have changed for whatever reason you probably also need to change your cooking and shopping habits. If your teenage son and his friends are no longer raiding the refrigerator on a daily basis your life has changed and you will need to change your shopping and cooking habits or you will be tempted to overeat rather than let food go to waste. Consulting with your dietitian can help you identify the dietary changes needed to make you the master of this situation.

It is a good idea to consult with your dietitian whenever you experience a major lifestyle event. Marriage, divorce, a death in the family, or a job change can affect your eating habits and your glucose control. Retirement can also have a major effect on your diet. This is true for most people not only when they retire but also when a spouse retires.

A dietitian can be a powerful ally in learning how to eat to maintain good glucose control and good health. It is just as important for people who have diabetes to have their own personal dietitian as it is for them to have a personal physician. Just as you see your physician periodically to make sure your diabetes is in good control, plan to see your dietitian annually to maintain good glucose control and good "waist" control.

Will My Insurance Pay a Dietitian?

The answer to that question is changing as this book goes to press. I am pleased to report the changes appear to be positive. More and more private insurance health plans are recognizing the value of medical nutrition therapy and its contribution to blood glucose control. Organized efforts to educate legislators and decision makers about the value of preventive care have resulted in improved coverage. Preventive services, including diabetes self-management that includes medical nutrition therapy, have been recognized and included in the 1997 Medicare Reform.

Individual insurance coverage will vary from company to company and state to state. The American Diabetes Association, The American Dietetic Association, and the American Association of Diabetes Educators have joined forces to work for uniform insurance coverage in every state. However, insurance coverage is a state issue and consequently can vary from state to state. Contact your insurance company and ask if diabetes medical nutrition therapy is a covered service. If the services you need in order to maintain good glucose are not available, ask your provider or employer why they are not covered. Insurers want to maintain their customer base and they do this through customer satisfaction. When dealing with legislators, whether local or national, it is important to have your facts straight and to be persistent. Contact your local American Diabetes Association office and ask about insurance in your state. (Your local office may be reached by calling 1–800–342–2383.) Ask your dietitian if insurance covers his or her services. Many times if they write a letter explaining why you need the service, an insurance company may cover it. More and more managed care organizations are becoming convinced of the cost benefits of preventive treatment.

CHAPTER 14

Can You "Live" with Diabetes?

Some people think the diagnosis of diabetes dooms them to a dreary existence, but it doesn't have to be that way. Positive lifestyle changes can benefit you and those around you as well. If you start a walking program and encourage a friend or family member to join you, both of you will benefit.

Over the years I have worked with many people who have type 2 diabetes. Just about all of them were devastated when first diagnosed; however, as they began to make the necessary lifestyle changes, many of them changed their tune. The reason for this is that the changes people make in order to self-manage their diabetes are the kinds of changes that make you feel better, and are the same things that everyone should do for a healthy lifestyle. Stop and think about it. If you are overweight and you lose 10 pounds you feel better physically because you have ten less pounds to move around, but more important, losing that 10 pounds gives most people a great psychological boost.

The same thing is true of physical activity, because once you start to become more active you generally have more, not less, energy. If you take physical activity to the exercise level, you may experience some sore muscles for a few days, but once you have established a routine you will feel better. Remember chapter 2, where we defined the difference between physical activity and exercise. For our purposes physical activity is moving more, whether it be parking farther from the entrance to the shopping mall or washing the dishes rather than using the dishwasher. Exercise is sustained physical activity where you actually increase your heart rate and work up a sweat.

I do not want to give you the impression that all of these changes are easy, and I often compare losing weight to quitting smoking. We know that nicotine is addictive and that it is difficult for most people to quit smoking once they have established the habit. We also know it is easier for a person to quit if they are not exposed to cigarette smoke at all and much more difficult to quit if you are around people who smoke. For just a moment apply that same principle to eating. It is easier not to eat pie or whatever your favorite food is if there is no pie in your house, so frequently people like me will advise people who want to lose weight to get rid of the foods they find they will overeat. One problem here is that unlike tobacco, society as a whole sees pie, cookies, candy, and chips as "good" and consequently they are very available. I have never seen a restaurant with a "no dessert" section where people who were watching their weight did not have to be exposed to secondhand temptation.

While it may be possible to restrict desserts and other sweets, there are some people who do not necessarily like sweets, they just like food. And it is impossible to give up food altogether, as one might give up smoking or alcohol completely. We do not ask a smoker who is trying to quit to have just one cigarette three times a day, nor do we ask someone who is trying to abstain from alcohol to have just a small drink three times a day, but that is exactly what we do ask of someone who needs to lose weight.

My point in all of this is to say that I know weight loss is extremely difficult and that anyone who is successful at losing weight needs to be congratulated. When a smoker quits and reports this to his or her health care provider everyone is happy and lavishes well-deserved praise upon the ex-smoker. They have made a monumental step in lowering their risk for a variety of diseases. The person who loses 10 pounds is also reducing their risk for several diseases, but unfortunately in our society instead of being congratulated on their success, that person is usually told to lose 10 more.

Neither you nor I can change the world and the way everyone thinks about weight, but you can change your own thinking about your own weight. We have discussed all sorts of weight loss strategies, but what we are really talking about here is an attitude. If you measure your weight loss success by measuring your blood glucose control you will be far less sensitive to what others think about your progress and will be able to congratulate yourself every time you check your glucose and find it in the appropriate range.

If you concentrate on making more healthful food choices, like substituting whole grains for refined grains or trying to incorporate more fresh fruits and vegetables in your diet, you are making a better choice not only for yourself but also for all the people in your family for whom you prepare meals. Always remember that food that is good for the person with diabetes to eat is good for the whole family. So we are back to attitude again. Instead of thinking you are the reason your whole family has to give up something, think about the positive benefits for those people in your household whose food choice options you have changed for the better.

For years, people with diabetes were given very specific advice about what to eat and what foods to avoid and this was different from the advice given to people with heart disease. Thank goodness those days are gone. While people with diabetes have special needs about timing or matching medication and food, the types of food recommended are the same for everyone, whether they have one of these diseases or not. Everyone needs fiber, whole grains, fresh fruits, vegetables, and sources of low-fat protein in their daily meal plan. So as a result of your improved food selection the whole family is benefiting from your making more healthful food choices.

Remember Molly and her lifelong struggles with weight? She is making progress and measuring that progress with a different scale. She changed her thinking about weight after she developed diabetes, or at least she is working on this attitude change, since this is a lifelong struggle. She is really trying to focus on her health rather than on an "ideal" body weight, and this is not an easy task in a world that is obsessed with thinness. Molly uses her blood glucose monitor regularly to check her progress.

The holidays were the first major challenge Molly faced since her diagnosis, and she was determined to overcome obstacles that she thought might undermine her goals for making lifestyle changes. The holidays were the one time of the year she cooked, and she always prepared traditional family favorites, but this year she analyzed the recipes and made some modifications. These foods will never be considered low-calorie; however, they are lower in calories than they have ever been before, and much to her amazement no one knew the difference.

The other tactic Molly used to help her cope with the holidays was to spend more time concentrating on decor and less time on food. She decided this was the year to concentrate on crafts rather than cookies and used her needlework skills to make a new holiday tablecloth. She also told her family and friends that they needed to support her lifestyle changes and to respect her decision when she said "no, thank you" to food.

Life is different in her home now for everyone. She and her husband go for a walk on most evenings after dinner and find that this change has lots of hidden benefits. They see it as their quality time to talk, uninterrupted by other family members, phone calls, or television. It is something they agreed upon and they motivate each other; for example, if Molly has had a hard day and is inclined to skip her evening walk her husband encourages her to join him and reminds her that she will feel better as a result of her effort. Molly is very fortunate to have a supportive husband and he is reaping the benefits of their mutual lifestyle changes, as they both have found they can wear clothes that were too tight 6 months ago.

Sam has been thin for his entire 73 years and his physician decided that after 3 months of trying to control his blood glucose with changes in eating and increases in activity he needed additional help and prescribed Amaryl, a sulfonylurea, once a day. At first Sam was distraught at the idea of taking medication, as he felt that if he had really eaten right and exercised enough he could have controlled his blood glucose without medication. His physician explained to him that diabetes is a progressive disease and that most people will need medication at some stage of the disease and will ultimately need to switch to insulin therapy to maintain glucose control.

Sam understood that his medication and food needed to work together, so he revisited his dietitian to make sure he was doing everything right. Amaryl is a medication that should be taken once a day at breakfast or at the first meal of the day. As with any drug that lowers blood glucose, I explained that there is always a risk for hypoglycemia, particularly if you take your medication and skip your meals. This wasn't a particular problem for Sam, as he followed a pretty standard routine from day to day, but to be organized and cautious I advised him to purchase a commercial preparation to treat hypoglycemia. He said he would buy this and keep some in his car as well as in the house so that in the unlikely event that he experienced hypoglycemia he would be prepared.

Sam and I also talked about the food he was selecting for meals and snacks. He reported that he liked following the food pyramid I had given him at his first visit and that he had used magnets to post it on his refrigerator to remind himself to eat at least one thing from the bottom three levels at each meal. That advice made meal planning much easier for him and that was important, since this was a recently acquired skill.

We also reviewed portion sizes. Sam said he had made a chart that told him how much of an uncooked food he needed to weigh to get just the right ready-to-eat portion size. He reported that he was beginning to enjoy cooking and was getting more adventuresome in his use of spices and herbs to enhance the flavor of foods. His cooking skills have progressed to the point where he even invited some old friends to dinner. Life was returning to normal. He regretted not having learned to cook much earlier in life, as this would have been a perfect hobby to share with his wife.

Sam was becoming more realistic in his shopping habits as well. After having had to throw away what he could not eat from the giant packages, he had learned the hard way that the large economy size is not always a bargain. He also had trouble with produce: he would purchase the family-size packages because it was cheaper than the loose produce. I suggested that he reconsider and buy one or two produce items at a time, like one carrot, a single potato, apple, or banana rather than prepackaged amounts. Even if you pay a little more, it will be more economical in the long run to buy only what you can eat and not pay for something that will spoil before you can eat it. Remember, the "waist" to consider is yours.

Diabetes had a major impact on Chef Pete's life. He accepted my challenge to modify recipes to reduce calories, sugar, fat, and salt and to create new recipes incorporating these principles, and now he is writing a cookbook! His light gourmet cookbook will include recipes for everything from soup to nuts and will have a section on party foods. One of his big emphases is presentation. Pete firmly believes we eat with our eyes, and if the food is attractively arranged on the plate it will taste better.

One of the things he tells me is that he is going to include a section on phytochemicals. He is developing recipes that feature functional foods and plans to include some that use tofu. He has worked hard on finding ways to reduce fat while retaining flavor, such as using herbs and spices to enhance flavors and vegetable and fruit purees in place of high-fat sauces.

His efforts have paid off personally, as he is the proud loser of 20 pounds and attributes this to his new style of eating. He does admit that he has cut his portion size in addition to modifying recipes. I know he joined a health club and is exercising, actually working up a sweat two or three times a week. His wife is happy too—as she lost 10 pounds simply as a result of supporting Pete.

Pete has also made some changes in his restaurants. Now that food labeling applies to restaurants, Pete has decided that he cannot make any statements on the menus that would be subject to the new rules, as the written backup materials would be difficult to provide. He did make some changes in his preparation methods that have lowered fat and calories, but he didn't advertise these changes. A side benefit of some of these changes has actually been lower food costs, as fat is expensive. He also added a statement to his restaurant menus saying that if a customer has special needs or special requests the kitchen staff would do their best to honor them.

Molly, Sam, and Pete are all doing well in their quest to control their diabetes. It is my sincere desire that you too will take an active role in managing your diabetes and live life to the fullest.

Diabetes Cookbooks

Another Choice: Easy, Lowfat Vegetarian Cooking

40 pages
IDC Publishing
888–637–2675

The Carbohydrate Counting Cookbook

Tami Ross, R.D., C.D.E., and Patti Geil, R.D., C.D.E.
208 pages, ISBN: 0–471–34671–3
John Wiley & Sons, Inc.
Available at bookstores everywhere.
$14.95

Complete Quick and Hearty Diabetic Cookbook

272 pages
American Diabetes Association
800–232–6733
$12.95

Diabetic Low-Fat & No-Fat Meals in Minutes

M. J. Smith, R.D.
356 pages, ISBN: 0–471–34678–0
John Wiley & Sons, Inc.
Available at bookstores everywhere.
$19.95

Flavorful Seasons Cookbook

Robyn Webb
452 pages
American Diabetes Association
800–232–6733
$14.95

More Flavor, Less Fat

36 pages
IDC Publishing
888–637–2675
$3.50

No Fuss Diabetes Recipes

Jackie Boucher, M.S., R.D., C.D.E.;
Marcia Hayes, M.P.H., R.D.;
Jane Stephenson, R.D., C.D.E.
192 pages, ISBN: 0–471–34794–9
John Wiley & Sons, Inc.
Available at bookstores everywhere.
$15.95

Quick and Easy Diabetic Recipes for One

Kathleen Stanley, C.D.E., R.D., M.S.E.D.,
and Connie C. Crawley, M.S., R.D., L.D.
129 pages
American Diabetes Association
800–232–6733
$12.95

Suggested Reading

American Diabetes Association Complete Guide to Diabetes

446 pages
American Diabetes Association
800–232–6733
$29.95

The American Dietetic Association's Complete Food and Nutrition Guide

Roberta Larson Duff, M.S., R.D., C.F.C.S.
637 pages, ISBN: 0–471–34659–4
John Wiley & Sons, Inc.
Available at bookstores everywhere.
$24.95

Caring for the Diabetic Soul

213 pages
American Diabetes Association
800–232–6733
$8.95

Diabetes: A Guide to Living Well

Ernest Lowe and Gary Arsham, M.D., Ph.D.
384 pages, ISBN: 0–471–34677–2
John Wiley & Sons, Inc.
Available at bookstores everywhere.
$14.95

Diabetes 101

Betty Page Brackenridge, M.S., R.D., C.D.E., and
Richard O. Dolinar, M.D.
224 pages, ISBN: 0–471–34675–6
John Wiley & Sons, Inc.
Available at bookstores everywhere.
$12.95

Exchange Lists for Meal Planning

32 pages
American Diabetes Association
800–232–6733
Single copy: $1.75

The First Step in Diabetes Meal Planning

pamphlet
American Diabetes Association
800–342–2383
Single copy, free

The Fitness Book for People with Diabetes

149 pages
American Diabetes Association
800–232–6733
$16.95

How to Get Great Diabetes Care

Irl B. Hirsch, M.D.
180 pages
American Diabetes Association
800–232–6733
$11.95

Managing Type 2 Diabetes

Arlene Monk, R.D., L.D., C.D.E.,
Jan Pearson, B.A.N., R.N., C.D.E.,
Priscilla Hollander, M.D., Ph.D.,
Richard Bergenstal, M.D.
192 pages
IDC Publishing
888–637–2675
$11.95

A Touch of Diabetes

Lois Jovanovic-Peterson, M.D.,
Charles M. Peterson, M.D.,
Morton B. Stone
192 pages, ISBN: 0471–34754–x
John Wiley & Sons, Inc.
Available at bookstores everywhere.
$13.95

Weight Management for Type II Diabetes

Jackie Labat, M.S., R.D., C.D.E., and
Annette Maggi, M.S., R.D.
224 pages, ISBN: 0–471–34750–2
John Wiley & Sons, Inc.
Available at bookstores everywhere.
$12.95

Helpful Organizations

American Association of Diabetes Educators
100 West Monroe Street
Fourth Floor
Chicago, Illinois 60603–1901
312–899–0040

The American Association of Diabetes Educators is a multidisciplinary organization of health professionals who teach people with diabetes.

AADE was established in 1973 as the organization dedicated solely to the needs of diabetes educators. Through educational programs and publications, legislative initiatives and leadership development, AADE has worked to promote the role of the diabetes educator and to advance the quality of diabetes education and care.

American Diabetes Association
1701 North Beauregard Street
Alexandria, Virginia 22311
800–342–2383

The American Diabetes Association is the nation's leading nonprofit health organization providing diabetes research, information, and advocacy. Founded in 1940, it was reorganized in 1969 to increase its ability to serve the public. Today, staff and volunteers in more than 800 communities conduct programs in all 50 states and the District of Columbia.

The mission of the organization is to prevent and cure diabetes, and to improve the lives of all people affected by diabetes. To fulfill this mission, the American Diabetes Association funds research, publishes scientific findings, and provides information and other services to people with diabetes, their families, health care professionals, and the public.

The American Dietetic Association
216 West Jackson Boulevard
Chicago, Illinois 60606–6995
312–899–0040
800–366–1655

The American Dietetic Association (ADA) is the world's largest organization of food and nutrition professionals, with nearly 70,000 members in 57 countries. ADA members, 80 percent of whom are registered dietitians (R.D.s) or dietetic technicians, registered (D.T.R.s), serve the public by offering prevention and wellness services and medical nutrition therapy. Dietetics practitioners work in a variety of settings, including health care, public health, food service, business, communications, research, education, and private practice.

Guided by a Strategic Framework focusing on vital Public, Policy, and Member Initiatives, ADA and its Foundation

(ADAF) work to enhance the nutritional well-being of the public on many fronts. Targeted consumer education campaigns show key audiences how to make healthful food choices. Government relations efforts help advance health-promoting legislation, and a wide range of programs and resources empower ADA members to positively affect the nutritional health of the publics they serve.

Useful Web Sites

American Association of Diabetes Educators
http://www.aadenet.org

American Diabetes Association
http://www.diabetes.org/

American Dietetic Association
http://www.eatright.org

Centers for Disease Control and Prevention
http://www.cdc.gov/diabetes

Department of Veterans Affairs
http://www.va.gov/health/diabetes/

Health Resources and Services Administration
http://www.hrsa.dhhs.gov

Indian Health Service
     http://www.ihs.gov

Juvenile Diabetes Foundation International
     http://www.jdfcure.org

National Diabetes Education Program
     http://ndep.nih.gov

National Institute of Diabetes and Digestive and Kidney Disease
of the National Institutes of Health
     http://www.niddk.nih.gov

Food Composition—USDA's Handbook 8 in searchable format
     http://www.nal.usda.gov/fnic/foodcomp/

USDA/FDA Foodborne Illness Education Information Center
     http://www.nal.usda.gov/fnic/foodborne/

USDA's Food and Nutrition Information Center
     http://www.nalusda.gov/fnic/

Healthy People 2010
     http://www.health.gov/healthypeople/

Index

Acarbose, 189, 192
acesulfame K, 97
Actos, 189, 194
alcohol consumption, 110–111, 209
Alitame, 98
allicin, 176
alpha-glucosidase inhibitors, 189, 192–193
Amaryl, 189, 191
American Association of Diabetes Educators, 206, 223
American Diabetes Association (ADA)
  contact information, 92, 206, 224
  Exchange Lists for Meal Planning, 26, 68, 78, 83, 90–94, 129–132
  as information resource, 26, 33, 40–41, 78, 206, 224

Nutrition Recommendations for Persons with Diabetes, 88
American Dietetic Association
  contact information, 224
  as information resource, 90, 204, 224–225
  National Center for Nutrition and Dietetics, 204
amylin, 196–197
antioxidants, 172–175
appetite suppressants, 25
appetizers, 81, 160
Apple Muffins, recipe for, 71–72
applesauce, in recipe modification, 115–117
aspartame, 97
Avandia, 189, 194
avocado, 107

Baked Tortilla Chips, recipe for, 55–56

balanced diet, 7–8, 18

Bayer Plus, 172

behavior modification, 23–24, 33–34, 72

beta-carotene, 170, 172–173, 179

beverages, 39, 47, 49–50, 62, 89

BIDS therapy, 195–196

biguanide, 189, 193–194

Bisquick, 147

blood glucose:
   control of, generally, 4, 12, 14, 17, 19, 27, 33, 90–91
   effect on food, 36
   improvement in, 21
   self-monitoring, 32–34, 39–40, 140–141

Blueberry Cobbler, recipes for, 145–148

borderline diabetes, 196

Bran Muffins recipes
   Fat-Free, 117–118
   Fat-Reduced, 116
   Modified, 115–116
   Original, 114–115

breads, 41, 52, 62, 63, 88

breakfast suggestions
   for calorie-counting diet, 28
   diabetes pyramid and 44
   sample menu, 15–16

broccoli, 174–175

Bufferin, 172

butter, 12, 45, 62, 106

B vitamins, 171

calorie-counting
   carbohydrates, 62–63
   diets, 25–28

fats, 60–61

food choices, 64–65

modified recipes, 68–73

proteins, 63–64

purpose of, 58–59

recipe modifications, 65–68

in very-low-calorie diets (VLCDs), 25–26

calories
   awareness of, 5, 8, 11, 16, 57–58
   burning of, 27
   counting, see calorie-counting
   defined, 58
   Nutrition Facts, on labels, 127–128

Campbell's soups, 153–154

cancer, prevention of
   antioxidants and, 172–175
   breast, 176
   healthy foods for the prevention of, 175–179
   stomach, 178

candy, 62–63, 99–101

canola oil, 107

caprenin, 113, 120

carbohydrates
   awareness of, 11, 16
   blood glucose, effect on, 62–63, 114
   breakdown of, 59
   in calorie-counting, 62–63
   Exchange List classifications, 91
   exchanges, 92–95
   importance of, 29
   low-carbohydrate diets, 28–30

Nutrition Facts, on labels,
     128–129
sources of, 62
cellulose, 113, 121
cereals, 15–16, 41, 62–63, 79,
     88, 137–138
cheating, 139, 142
cheese(s), 42, 69, 152
chicken
     calorie-counting diets, 27
     Coq au Vin recipe, 68–69
     portion size, 79
     preparation guidelines, 5, 48,
          159
     as protein source, 62
Chinese food, 48–50
chlorpropamide, 189, 190
chocolate candy, 62, 92,
     100–101, 142
cholesterol
     ADA dietary
          recommendations, 105
     defined, 109, 118
     dietary, 118
     effect of, 19, 21
     fat intake and, generally,
          107
     high-density lipoprotein
          (HDL), 107, 118
     low-density lipoprotein
          (LDL), 107, 110, 118,
          194
     physical need for, 109
     VLDL, 118
chromium deficiency, 171
chronic disease, 90
citrus peel, 176
Coca-Cola, 89
coconut oil, 106

comfort foods
     blood glucose levels and,
          140–141
     fat in, 148–152
     recipe modifications,
          143–148
     salt in, 152–154
     selection factors, 141–143
     sugar in, 144
convenience foods, 7, 14
cookbooks, listing of, 215–217
cooking guidelines
     family meals, 77
     meat and poultry, 79–80
     portion sizes, 80–81
     preparation, 17
cookware, 17
Coq au Vin, recipe for, 68–69
crab, 160
Cyclamate, 98

Daily Value, on labels
     health claim requirements,
          138
     nutrient claims and, 135
     in Nutrition Facts, 126–128
dairy products, 6, 42, 52, 106
desserts, 208–209. See also
          specific types of desserts
Di'Gel, 172
Diabeta, 189, 191
diabetes
     physical impact of, 183, 190.
     prevalence of, 3
     See also hypoglycemia
diabetes pyramid
     levels of, 41–42, 46
     meal suggestions, 44–46
     purpose of, 41

Diabinese, 189, 190
dietary cholesterol, 118
dietary guidelines, 104–105
diet center programs, 30
dietitian
  appointments, frequency of,
    204–205
  Certified Diabetes Educator
    (C.D.E), 201, 203–204
  insurance coverage, 205–206
  location guidelines, 203–204
  need for, 201–203
  Registered Dietitian (R.D.),
    26, 203
  role of, 15, 26, 31
diets, overview
  calorie-counting, 26–28
  diet center programs, 30
  exchanges, 26
  fat gram, 29–30
  low-carbohydrate, 28–29
  very-low-calorie diets
    (VLCDs), 25–26
diglycerides, 113
dinner suggestions
  for calorie-counting diet, 28
  diabetes pyramid levels and,
    44
  food preparation, 5, 17
  sample menu, 18

eating habits
  change guidelines, 13–17
  food selections, 9–11
  frequency of meals, 27, 198
  impact of, generally, 8–9
  hypoglycemia and, 198
  portion size, 12, 15, 72

scheduling meals, 8, 12, 27
  for weight loss, 23–30
eating out
  custom prepared foods,
    166–167
  fats in, 163–164
  food preparation methods,
    nutrient value in, 158–163
  meal plan suggestions,
    160–162
  ordering guidelines, 157–158
  sharing meals, 166
  tipping guidelines, 167
  truthful menus, 164
eggs, 42, 59, 62
Eli Lilly and Company, 186
empty calories, 76
emulsifiers, 113, 120
Equal, 97, 146
ethnic foods, 12, 46–53. *See also*
    specific ethnic cuisines
exchange diet, 26
Exchange Lists for Meal Planning,
    26, 68, 78, 83, 90–93,
    129–131
exercise
  blood glucose levels, effect
    on, 34, 37
  cholesterol level and, 110
  fat intake and, 105
  guidelines for, 22–23

fast food, 45
fat(s)
  calorie-counting and, 60–61
  cholesterol level and, 107,
    109–110
  content, awareness of, 14

in cooking, 60–61
defined, 118–121
intake guidelines, 104–106
metabolism and, 27, 109
physical impact of, 28–29
physical need for, 104
recipe modifications for,
    115–118, 148–152
replacers, 112–114, 120–121
sources of, 62
storage in the body, 59
types of, 106–107, 110–111,
    118–119
Fat-Free Bran Muffins, 117
fat-free foods, defined, 61
Fat-Reduced Bran Muffins, 116
fat gram diet, 29
fat replacers
caloric, 120–121
noncaloric, 120
overview, 112–114
fatty acids
defined, 118
omega-3, 111–112, 119
trans-, 107–109, 119
festive occasions, 9–10
First Step in Diabetes Meal
    Planning, The, 33, 41,
    132
fish, 26, 42, 48–49, 51,
    110–111, 159. See also
    specific types of fish
fish oil supplements, 111
flavenoids, 178
flavorings, in recipe
    modifications, 144
Food and Drug Administration
    (FDA), regulation by, 84,
97–98, 123, 129, 131–132,
    135–136, 186
Food Guide Pyramid
benefits of, 8
development of, 41
diabetes pyramid, see diabetes
    pyramid
ethnic foods, 46–53
lesson of, 53
snacks, 54–56
food measurement, 79–80
food records, 37
Food Safety and Inspection
    Service (FSIS), 123, 132,
    135
food safety, label information,
    see label-reading
food storage, 83–85
fried foods, 49, 157–159
frozen foods, 10
fructose, 88
fruit(s)
Apple Muffin recipe, 71–72
apples, 10–11
blood glucose, effect on, 81
as carbohydrate source,
    62–63
citrus peel, 176
in diabetes pyramid, 41–42
in ethnic foods, 49–50, 52
grapes, 81, 177
limes, 170
oranges, 11
portion size of, 81
serving size
    recommendations, 130
watermelon, 81
functional foods, 169

garlic, 176–177
glimepiride, 189, 191
glipizide, 189, 190
Glucophage, 189, 193–194
Glucotrol/Glutotrol XL, 189, 190–191
glyburide, 189, 191
Glynase PresTab, 189, 191
Glyset, 189, 192
goal-setting
    realistic, 13
    for weight loss, 20, 22, 32
grains, in diabetes pyramid, 41
Grandma's Blueberry Cobbler, 145
Greek cuisine, 12, 51–52
grocery shopping, 24, 84–85, 213
guar, 113, 121
gums, 113, 121

hamburgers, 8, 44
HDL (high-density lipoprotein) cholesterol, 107, 110, 118
health claims
    FDA regulations, 135–137
    on labels, generally, 135–138
    on restaurant menus, 164–165
healthful foods
    benefits of, 210
    broccoli, 175
    citrus peel, 176
    garlic, 176–177
    grapes, 177
    tea, 178
    soybeans, 177–178
    tomatoes, 178
    vegetables, 175–176

health insurance coverage, 205–206
Healthy Request soups, 154
heart disease, 90, 111, 136, 176, 178
high-calorie foods, 10, 142
holidays, 8–9
Humalog, 186
hydrogenated fat, 118
hydrogenated starch hydrolysates, 99–100
hypertension, 136, 152
hypoglycemia
    treatment for, 193, 198–199
    triggers of, 185, 193, 197–198

ice cream, 94, 99, 106
Indian cuisine, 52–53
information resources
    American Diabetes Association, 26, 33, 40, 41, 78
    Exchange List for Meal Planning, 26, 68, 78, 83, 90–93, 129–131
    The First Step in Diabetes Meal Planning, 33, 41, 132
    professional organizations, 223–225
    suggested reading, 219–221
    U.S. Department of Agriculture (USDA), 77–78
    web sites, 227–228
ingredients section, on labels, 124
injections, insulin, 185–187

insulin
　analog action, 186
　animal action, 184
　effect of, 22, 181–187
　human action, 185
　injections, 185–187
　oral medications and, 188,
　　195–196
　types of, 185–187
Internet web sites, as
　　information resource,
　　227–228
isomalt, 99
Italian cuisine, 12, 50–51

Jenny Craig, 30
junk food junkies, 12

kitchen scale, 79–80

label-reading
　health claims, 135–138
　importance of, 123
　ingredients, 124
　nutrient content claims,
　　132–135
　nutrition facts, 124–129
　serving size, 129–132
lactitol, 99
lard, 60, 62, 106, 116
LDL (low-density lipoprotein)
　　cholesterol, 107, 110, 118,
　　194
lifestyle changes
　case illustrations, 31–39,
　　210–214
　importance of, 207–210
light foods, defined, 134

limonoids, 176
lipid, defined, 118
lipoprotein, defined, 118
liquid diets, 26
lispro insulin, 186
Lita, 120
lite foods, defined, 134, 165
liver function, 197
lobster, 110, 159
low-calorie foods, 135
low-fat, fat-free debate, 61
low-fat foods, defined, 165
low-sodium foods, 135
luncheon meats, 134
lunch suggestions
　in calorie-counting diet, 28
　diabetes pyramid levels and,
　　44–45
lycopene, 178–179

Maalox, 172
McDonald's McLean Deluxe,
　　164
magnesium, 172
maintenance, after weight loss,
　　26
maltodextrin, 121
mannitol, 98–99
margarine, 12, 45, 62, 108, 118,
　　149
marinades, low-fat, 151
meal-planning basics
　balance, 7–8
　dinner, 5
　eating habits, 8–12
　moderation, 6–7
　sample menus, 17–18
　variety, 6

meat(s)
  ethnic foods, 49, 52
  Exchange List
    recommendations, 91
  as fat, 62
  fat reduction strategies, 106,
    150
  hamburgers, 8, 44
  lamb, 52
  luncheon, 134
  meatballs, 6
  portion size, 79
  as protein source, 62
  steak, 45, 59, 159
  in very-low-calorie diets
    (VLCDs), 26
medications
  alpha-glucosidase inhibitors,
    189,192–193
  appetite suppressants, 25
  biguanide, 189, 193–194
  future directions, 196–197
  hypoglycemia and, 197–199
  insulin, 181–187, 195–196
  meglitinide, 189, 191
  oral, 187–196
  sulfonylureas, 189–190
  thiazolidinediones, 189,
    194–195
Mediterranean diet, 51, 60
meglitinide, 191
menus, sample, 17–18
Metformin, 189, 193–194
Mexican cuisine, 12, 46–47
Micronase, 189, 191
microwave cooking, 10, 17, 35
Middle Eastern cuisine, 12
miglitol, 189, 192

milk and milk products
  as fat, 62
  in diabetes pyramid, 42, 52–53
  effects of, 6, 128–129
  portion size, 106
  as protein source, 62
  recipe modifications with, 71,
    147, 150
moderation, importance of, 6–7,
  12
modified food starch, 121
Modified Bran Muffins, 115–116
monoglycerides, 113
monosaccharides, 192
monounsaturated fats, 106–107,
  116, 119
Mylanta, 172

National Cancer Institute, 173
Neotame, 98
neuropathy, 196
Novo Nordisk (Novolog), 186
nutraceutical, 169
NutraSweet, 97
nutrient content claims, on
  labels, 132–135
Nutrition Education and
  Labeling Act (1990), 135,
  164
Nutrition Facts, on labels
  information in, 124–129
  serving size and, 130

Oatrim, 121
obesity, 19, 110–111
oils, 51, 53, 62, 107
Olean, 113, 120
Olestra, 113

olive oil, 51, 52, 60, 107, 116
olives, 107
omega-3 fatty acids, 111–112, 119
oral medications, 187–196
Original Bran Muffins, 114–115
Orinase, 190
osteoporosis, 177
Overeaters Anonymous, 30
overeating, 7, 9

pancreas, function of, 183, 190
pasta, 6, 50, 53, 62–63, 83
pastries, 60, 63
peanut butter, 42
Phillips' Milk of Magnesia, 172
physical activity, 22–23, 208
Physicians Health Study, 173
phytochemicals, 169–170, 176–177, 213
pioglitazone hydrochloride, 189, 194–195
pizza, 8, 34, 37–38, 45
polydextrose, 113, 121
polyunsaturated fats, 106–107, 119
pork, 48
portion size
    cooking guidelines, 77, 80
    exchanges, 93–94
    food storage suggestions, 83–85
    importance of, 12, 15, 72, 75, 82–85, 212
    in restaurants, 77–78
    USDA serving sizes and, 77
    weighing and measuring, 78–79

potatoes, 7, 12, 45
poultry, 26, 42, 49, 51, 62, 150–151
Prandin, 189, 191
Precose, 189, 192
processed foods, 10–11
protein(s)
    breakdown of, 59
    in fat gram diet, 29
    physical need for, 63–64
    sources, 8, 62

quercetin, 178

recipe modifications, see specific recipes
    fat content, 148–152
    salt content, 152–154
    sugar and, 144
recipes
    Apple Muffins, 71–72
    Coq au Vin, Pete's, 68–69
    Fat-Free Bran Muffins, 117
    Fat-Reduced Bran Muffins, 116
    Grandma's Blueberry Cobbler, 145
    Modified Blueberry Cobbler, 146–148
    Modified Bran Muffins, 115–116
    Original Bran Muffins, 114–115
    Salsa, 54–55
    Spaghetti Sauce, 82–83
    Stuffed Zucchini Squash, 70–71
    Tortilla Chips, Baked, 55–56

recordkeeping, blood glucose
    levels, 36–37, 198
reduced-calorie foods, 164–165
Repaglinide, 189, 191
restaurants, *see* eating out
Resveratrol, 177
retinopathy, 196
rice, 27, 49, 51, 80
rosiglitazone, 194–195

saccharin, 96–97
salad(s), 5–7
salad dressings, 5, 158
salatrim, 113, 120
salmon, 112, 164
Salsa, recipe for, 54–55
salt content, 14
sardines, 112
saturated fats, 106, 116, 119
sauces
    healthy benefits of, 170
    Spaghetti Sauce recipe,
        82–83
    types of, 50, 53, 69
seafood, *see* fish
seasonings, 48, 53, 213
scheduling meals, 8, 12, 27, 198
self-management, importance
    of, 202
self-monitoring, blood glucose
    levels, 32–34, 39–40,
        140–141
serving size, *see* portion size
    on labels, 129–132
    USDA recommendations, 77
shrimp, 110
Simplesse, 120
smoking, health effects of, 208

snacks
    baked tortilla chips, recipe
        for, 55–56
    blood glucose levels, effect
        on, 35
    on calorie-counting diet, 27
    diabetes pyramid and, 44,
        54–56
    salsa recipe, 54–55
soda, 39, 62, 89
sodium intake, *see* salt
sorbitol, 98–99
soul food, 47–48
soup, 153–154, 162–163
sour cream, 45
soybeans, 177–178
soy and soy products, 113,
    177–178
soy milk, 49–50
starches, *see* pasta; potatoes
steamed foods, 49, 158–159, 175
Stuffed Zucchini Squash, recipe
    for, 70–71
sucralose, 97–98
sugar(s)
    alcohols, 98–100
    breakdown of, 87–88
    effect of, 53, 88–89
    exchanges, 92–95
    food selection and, 91–95
    informed choices, 100–101
    label-reading, 124
    replacers, 96–98
    simple, 192
sugar diabetes, 87
sugar-free foods, 101
sugar substitutes, 146, 148. *See
    also* sweeteners

sulfonylureas, 189, 190, 196
support groups, 30
Sweet'n Low, 96
sweeteners, 88, 99, 148
Sweet One, 97
Swiss Sweet, 97
syringes, 182

table sugar, 53, 88, 193
tasters, 13–14
test kits, home blood glucose,
    39
thiazolidinediones, 189,
    194–195
tolazamide, 189, 190
tolbutamide, 189, 190
Tolinase, 189, 190
tortillas, 46–47
Trailblazer, 120
trans-fatty acids, 107–109,
    119
triglycerides, 19, 21, 110–111
tuna, 112
turkey, 62

U.S. Department of Agriculture
    (USDA)
    Handbook 8 on the
        Composition of Foods—Raw,
        Processed, Prepared, 170
    recommendations and
        regulations by, 77–78,
        104–105, 123
    vitamin recommendations,
        179
U.S. Department of Health and
    Human Services (HHS),
    105

variety in diet, importance of,
    6, 18
veal scallopini, 66
vegetable fat, 108
vegetable oil, 60
vegetables
    as appetizers, 81
    benefits of, 5–9, 17, 27,
        175
    as carbohydrate, 62–63
    in diabetes pyramid levels,
        41–42, 44–45
    ethnic foods, 47–52
    as snacks, 35
very-low-calorie diets (VLCDs),
    25–26
vitamins and supplements
    antioxidants, 172–175
    chromium, 171
    in fat, 104
    in healthful foods, examples
        of, 175–179
    importance of, 171–172
    magnesium, 172
    nutrient claims, 135
    USDA recommendations,
        179
    vitamin C, 170, 172–175
    vitamin E, 175

weight loss
    case illustration, 31–39
    commitment to, 209
    as goal, 12, 14
    research on, 20–21
    strategies for, see weight loss
        strategies
    success stories, 210–214

weight loss strategies
  appetite suppressants, 25
  behavior modification,
    23–24
  calorie-counting diets, 26–28
  exchange diets, 26
  fat gram diets, 29–30
  generally, 21–22
  low-carbohydrate diets, 28–30
  physical activity, 22–23, 208

very-low-calorie diets
  (VLCDs), 25–26
wine, 177
wontons, 48–49

xylitol, 98–99

yogurt, 42, 52

Z-trim, 120